WORSHIP

Karyn Henley

Standard PUBLISHING

CINCINNATI, OHIO

WORSHIP

The foundation for loving God

Karyn Henley

FOUNDATIONS CURRICULUM

Published by Standard Publishing, Cincinnati, Ohio
A division of Standex International Corporation

Credits
Cover design by Brian Fowler
Interior design by Jeff Richardson
Cover and inside illustrations by Ed Koehler
Project editors, Jim Eichenberger, Ruth Frederick, Linda Ford, Bruce Stoker

09 08 07 06 05 04 03   8 7 6 5 4
ISBN 0-7847-1217-4
Printed in the United States of America

TABLE OF CONTENTS

INTRODUCTION

The Irish poet William Butler Yeats once said, "Education is not the filling of a pail, but the lighting of a fire." In the first temple, the tent of meeting, there was a lampstand. God's instructions were, "Tell the people of Israel to bring you pure olive oil for the lampstand, so it can be kept burning continually. . . . Aaron and his sons will keep the lamps burning in the Lord's presence day and night" (Exodus 27:20, 21, NLT). Today we are God's temple (1 Corinthians 3:16). And our passion, our living love for the Lord, keeps our lampstand burning before him. (See Revelation 2:4, 5.) Our job in the spiritual education of children is to light a fire, a living, growing love for God within them.

The Foundations curriculum can help light that fire. Each of our students is a temple of God. So the goal of the Foundations curriculum is to construct within children the essential foundations upon which they can build (and sustain) a loving, thriving relationship with the Lord. To do this, the Foundations curriculum provides a thorough, step-by-step, in-depth exploration of the following foundations.

Quarter 1: Studying the Bible, The Foundation for Knowing God

Quarter 2: Salvation, The Foundation for Living with God

Quarter 3: Prayer, The Foundation for Growing Closer to God

Quarter 4: Worship, The Foundation for Loving God

This curriculum is intended for use with students in third through fifth grades. Each quarter is independent of the others, so they can be taught in any order. In fact, each quarter can be used as a single unit to fill in a 13-week study at any time of the year and can be followed or preceded by any other curriculum of your choice.

The following arrangement is a suggestion showing how the Foundations Curriculum can be taught in one year. Studying the Bible (September–November), Salvation (December–February), Prayer (March–May), Worship (June–August).

WALK THROUGH A WEEK

SCRIPTURE AND GOAL

The session begins with a Scripture and a simple goal. You may use the Scripture as a memory verse if you wish, or you may use it to support the theme for the day, reading the Scripture when you gather for the first prayer.

INTRODUCTORY ACTIVITY

You can begin your introductory activity as soon as the first student arrives, guiding others to join you as they come into your room. This activity serves two purposes. First, it gives the students something fun to do from the first moment they arrive. Second, it starts thoughts and conversations about the theme of the session. Talking is encouraged. Questions are welcome. Get to know your students. Make it your goal to discover something interesting and special about each one. Let them know that their mission is to discover more about God and about how they can get to know him better every day, so that God becomes their constant companion, their treasured friend, their awesome king.

DISCOVERY RALLY

Gather the students together as a group in preparation for the Discovery Centers.

What's the Good Word? This is a time to read the Scripture for the day. You may also sing a few songs if you want.

Challenge. This is a time to introduce the students to the theme for the day by making challenging statements or asking challenging questions.

Prayer. Choose a student to lead a prayer of blessing for the day's activities, asking God to open your hearts and teach everyone present.

DISCOVERY CENTERS

You will need either one teacher/facilitator for each center, or clearly written instructions that tell the students what they are to do in the center.

The way your class uses Discovery Centers will depend on how much time you have and how many students there are in your class.

- If you have a few students, go together to as many centers as you can in the time you have.
- If you have more than ten students and lots of time, divide into three groups. Send one group to each center and let each group rotate to a different center as they finish the activity, so that each student gets to go to each center during Discovery Center time.

- If you have more than ten students, but little time, divide into groups of three. Number off, one to three in each group. Each student #1 goes to the first center, #2 goes to the second, #3 goes to the third. After each center has completed its activity, the original groups of three come back together again to tell each other what they learned in their centers.
- Or you may choose to let all three centers do the same activity. Choose the one or two activities that you think your students will enjoy most. Divide the students into groups for centers, and once they are there, do not rotate. Instead, let each group do the one or two activities you have chosen.

DEBRIEFING QUESTIONS

If you have time, gather together as a large group at the end of the session to ask and answer questions and discuss the theme and/or other issues on the students' minds.
Review the Scripture for the day.

PRAY

You or a student may close your class time in prayer.

SUGGESTED BIBLE STUDY HELPS

This is by no means a complete list. As you look for these, you will find others that may be just as interesting and helpful.

Bible Handbooks

What the Bible Is All About, Henrietta C. Mears (Gospel Light)

What the Bible Is All About for Young Explorers, Frances Blankenbaker (Gospel Light)

The International Children's Bible Handbook, Lawrence Richards (Word)

The Baker Bible Handbook for Kids, Marek Lugowski and Carol J. Smith (Baker)

New Unger's Bible Handbook: Student Edition, Merrill Unger (Moody)

Bible Encyclopedias

The Children's Bible Encyclopedia: The Bible Made Simple and Fun, Mark Water (Baker Books)

Bible Dictionaries

International Children's Bible Dictionary, Lynn Waller (Word)

The Baker Bible Dictionary for Kids (Baker)

Bible Fact Books

The Awesome Book of Bible Facts, Sandy Silverthorne (Harvest House)

The Baker Book of Bible People for Kids (Baker)

The Complete Book of Bible Trivia, J. Stephen Lang (Tyndale)

For Teachers and Older Students

Willmington's Bible Handbook, Harold L. Willmington (Tyndale)

Holman Topical Concordance (Holman Bible Publishers)

Holman Bible Dictionary (Holman Bible Publishers)

Children's Ministry Resource Edition (Thomas Nelson)

Manners and Customs in the Bible, Victor H. Matthews (Hendrickson)

What Is Worship?

Scripture

"God is spirit, and his worshipers must worship in spirit and in truth.   John 4:24

Goal

Learn that worship starts with an attitude of respect, awe, and love for God.

INTRODUCTION

Before the session begins, write each student's first and last name on an index card, one student's name per card, but scramble the letters of each name. On the back of each card, write the name of a candy bar, scrambling its letters (or if you want to stay away from sweets, use other types of snacks like fruits or crackers). Make sure you bring the corresponding number and types of snacks that you've written on the backs of the cards.

As the students arrive, give each one an index card containing the name of another student. Instruct the students to try to figure out who is holding their card. When a student finds her card, have her unscramble the name of the treat on the back, and then she can have that treat.

DISCOVERY RALLY

Gather the students together in a large group.

WHAT'S THE GOOD WORD?

Choose a student to read the Scripture for the day.

THE CHALLENGE

Ask: **Do any of you know what your name means?** Let them tell you the meanings of their names. **Does anyone know God's name? What are some of the names that we call God?** (Almighty, Most High God, Creator, Healer, Lord.) **What is worship? The word for "worship" in Hebrew means "to bow down." Worship is our heart attitude of "bowing down" to God. It is expressing our wonder and love for him.** Then tell the students that in their Discovery Groups today, they will learn more about worship and about who God is.

PRAYER

DISCOVERY GROUPS

1. GOD'S NAME

Before the session, print the letters YHWH in large block letters about 3 inches high and 2 inches wide on cardboard, poster board, or foam picnic plates. Then cut these letters out. If you anticipate having a large group of students, you may want two sets of these letters.

MATERIALS

markers; thick cardboard, poster board, Styrofoam plates; scissors; paper; crayons or colored pencils

DO: Give each student a piece of plain white paper. Have crayons or colored pencils available. Arrange the letters in order and let the students look at them. Ask them to say the word. Tell them that this is the name that God's people have called him since ancient times. Ask the students to place the letters underneath their papers and rub the crayon or colored pencils over the paper so that the letters show up. Since the stencil letters are separate from each other, students can use one letter at a time and share the letters.

DISCUSS: Even though we read the Bible in our own language, it was originally written in other languages. The Old Testament was written mostly in Hebrew, and the New Testament was written in Greek. The letters we have here represent the Hebrew letters that spell the name of God. If I were to spell the name of God using these four letters, what would you say is missing? (Vowels.) Hebrew doesn't have letters to represent vowel sounds the way English does. People reading Hebrew add the sounds of the missing vowels as they read aloud. So YHWH probably would have been pronounced "Yahweh." Later, people began to read the word as "Jehovah." However, the Hebrew people did not want to use God's name in vain, as one of the Ten Commandments told them, so instead of saying "Yahweh" or "Jehovah," they would say "Adonai" or "Lord." When people changed the Hebrew words into English words to get the Bible we read today, they also used the word "Lord." In fact, you can usually find the places where the Hebrew word YHWH was by looking for the word "Lord" in all capital letters. Turn to Genesis 15:1 in a KJV, NAS, NIV, or NLT version of the Bible and show them that "Lord" is in all capital letters, which means the Hebrew word was YHWH. The reason the Hebrew people and the Bible translators use this word is out of respect for God. They do not want to misuse God's name, so they use another word altogether. Worship is obeying God's command to "delight yourself in the LORD [YHWH]" (Psalm 37:4). It is expressing our respect, our wonder, and our love for God, to God.

2. A MURAL ABOUT THE MOST HIGH

Before the session, make a copy of the Names of God handouts and cut apart the names and descriptions. Attach the butcher paper to the wall. With a pencil, draw two horizontal lines along the length of the paper to separate it into three sections: top, middle, and bottom.

> **MATERIALS**
> copy of the Names of God handouts (pages 14–17), 8-foot length of butcher paper, pencil, crayons or markers

DO: Give the students crayons or markers. Then give each student a strip of paper containing a name of God and its description. Ask each student in your first group to choose a portion of the top section of the butcher paper to work in. (Your second group will work in the middle section, and your third group will work in the bottom section.) Tell the students to write on the mural the name of God that is shown on their paper. If it is a Hebrew or Greek name, they should write the

Hebrew or Greek name and the English name (for example: "El-Shaddai, Almighty God"). Then ask them to create a colorful design on the letters as well as in the section of the mural on which they are working.

DISCUSS: **True worship is not just what we do, such as praying to God or singing about God. Worship starts in our hearts. In fact, it is possible to do the right things in worship, and not really worship at all. How could that be?** Read, or ask a student to read, Matthew 15:8, 9. **What did Jesus mean when he said this? The starting place for all true worship is an attitude of respect for God.** Ask each student to read aloud the descriptive name of God that he wrote on the mural. If you have time, ask the students to read the rest of the description on their cards.

3. THE GREAT "I AM"

MATERIALS
modeling clay, wax paper, toothpicks, rolling pin

DO: Ask a student to read what God said his name was when he talked to Moses at the burning bush in Exodus 3:13, 14. Ask another student to read how God described himself to Moses in Exodus 33:18-23 and 34:4-7. Now give each student a 12-inch length of wax paper and a lump of modeling clay. Ask the students to roll or pat their clay into a 8-by-5-inch rectangle. Then give the students toothpicks and ask them to write the first of the Ten Commandments on the dough: "Do not worship any other gods besides me" (Exodus 20:3, NLT). Let these dry and send them home with the students.

DISCUSS: **How did God describe himself to Moses? What do you think God meant when he said his name was "I Am"? What does God mean when he tells us to worship him? Is it possible to worship God and not believe in him? Why does God say not to worship any gods besides him? How is it possible to worship something besides God? Worship is not just something we do, it is an attitude in our hearts. What kind of attitude would that be?** (It would be a respectful, loving attitude toward God. This attitude spills out into our expression of wonder and love for God, to God.)

If you have time, ask a student to read John 8:58. Read the last two words of that verse very carefully. **What did Jesus mean?**

Discoverers' Debriefing

DISCOVERERS' DEBRIEFING

If you have time to review, gather as a large group and discuss your young discoverers' findings. Ask the following questions:

- **What is the most interesting thing you discovered today?**
- **What did you learn today that you didn't know before?**
- **What is God's name?**
- **What are some of the descriptive names of God that are used in the Bible?**
- **Is it possible to pray and sing, doing the things we normally think of as worship, without really worshiping? Explain.**
- **What is the most important thing about worship?** (Loving and respecting God.)
- **Why does worship start with our attitude?**

Review the Scripture for today.

Pray, telling God that you love and respect him. Worship him in prayer, telling him that he is El-Shaddai, the Almighty. He is El-Elyon, the Most High. He is Elohim, the Creator. Tell him you worship him because of who he is.

Names of God

EL-SHADDAI "Almighty God"
This is the name that God used to describe himself to Abraham when he promised to make Abraham and his family a mighty nation (Genesis 17:1, 2).

EL-ELYON "Most High God"
Long ago, a priest from the city that would later become Jerusalem blessed Abraham in the name of El-Elyon (Genesis 14:19, 20). And Balaam (whose donkey once talked) blessed God's people by saying what "El-Elyon" told him to say (Numbers 24:15, 16). David also called God "the Most High" (2 Samuel 22:14).

EL-OLAM "Everlasting One"
Abraham worshiped God, calling him El-Olam (Genesis 21:33). And Moses wrote a prayer in which he called God El-Olam (Psalm 90:2).

EL-ROI "God Who Sees Me"
When Sarah's servant Hagar ran away, God sent an angel to tell her to go back home. After that, Hagar called God "El-Roi," because she knew God had seen her and was watching over her (Genesis 16:13).

ELOHIM "Creator God"
The Bible uses this name of God when it describes how God made people in his image (Genesis 1:26).

YAHWEH-YIREH "The Lord my Provider"
When God provided a ram for Abraham and Isaac to sacrifice on the mountain, Abraham even named the place "The Lord will Provide" (Genesis 22:14).

YAHWEH-NISSI "The Lord my Banner"

Long ago, armies carried their country's flag or banner into battle with them. The banner also flew over their camp. Moses called God "Yahweh-Nissi" after God's people had fought and won a battle over the enemy (Exodus 17:15). He was saying that God was with them in battle.

YAHWEH-MEKADDESH "The Lord Who Makes Holy"

"Holy" means "set apart" or "different." God is a different kind of being from all others. God told his people to have a special worship day set aside just for him: the Sabbath. God said that would help them remember that he is Yahweh-Mekaddesh, the Lord who makes his people holy (Exodus 31:13).

YAHWEH-SHALOM "The Lord Is Peace"

God's angel visited Gideon, and Gideon was afraid of the angel. But God said, "Do not be afraid. You will not die" (Judges 6:23, NLT). Then Gideon built an altar and worshiped God, calling him "Yahweh-Shalom" (Judges 6:24).

YAHWEH-SABAOTH "The Lord of Hosts"

This name means that God rules over all nations and over the whole universe. Jeremiah called God "Yahweh-Sabaoth" when God saved his life from men who were planning to kill him (Jeremiah 11:20).

YAHWEH-ROHI "The Lord my Shepherd"

This is the name David used to describe God in Psalm 23, "The Lord is my Shepherd; I have everything I need" (Psalm 23:1, NLT).

YAHWEH-SHAMMAH "The Lord Is There"

When the city of Jerusalem was built back again (after it had been torn down), Ezekiel called the city "Yahweh-Shammah," meaning that this city is a place where God is (Ezekiel 48:35).

ADONAI "Lord"

This word was used to address great people such as kings or masters. But when God's people used the word, they were honoring God as the highest King and Master, their Lord (Genesis 18:27; Psalm 16:2; 38:22; 54:4; 68:19). Sometimes they used "Adonai" in place of the word "Yahweh"; in fact, God's people came up with the name "Jehovah" by adding the vowel sounds of "Adonai" to the "unspeakable" name of God, "YHWH."

QANNA "Jealous"

God is jealous in a good way. When we want to give our attention, our hearts, our lives to something that cannot fulfill us like he can, he is jealous, and he wants us back. He loves us too much to let us give our lives to things that can't satisfy us. God told his people, "I, the Lord your God, am a jealous God who will not share your affection with any other god!" (Exodus 20:5, NLT; see also Exodus 34:14).

ANCIENT ONE

Daniel called God "the Ancient One" or "the Ancient of Days" when he saw a vision of God sitting on his throne as judge (Daniel 7:9, 13, 22).

ROCK

David called God "my Rock" (Psalm 19:14). Moses wrote a song that called God "the Rock" (Deuteronomy 32:18). And when Hannah was praising God after he had given her a baby (Samuel), she said, "There is no Rock like our God" (1 Samuel 2:2). This name of God means that he is dependable, strong, and everlasting.

FORTRESS

A fortress is a fort, a strong protection. David called God "my fortress" after God had saved David from Saul and all his other enemies (Psalm 18:2).

SHIELD

God told Abraham not to be afraid, because he was Abraham's shield (Genesis 15:1). God protects us just as a shield protects a soldier.

ABBA/FATHER The Aramaic word "Abba" can mean "Daddy." It shows a close loving relationship between father and child. Jesus used this word when he prayed to God (Mark 14:36), and the apostle Paul refers to God as Abba in Romans 8:15 and Galatians 4:6. Jesus told his followers to pray to God, calling God "Father" (Luke 11:1, 2). The Bible also calls God the "Father of Mercies" (2 Corinthians 1:3), the "Father of Lights" (James 1:17), and the "Father of Glory" (Ephesians 1:17).

WARRIOR Moses and Miriam sang a song after God had rescued them from the armies of Egypt. They said, "The Lord is a warrior" (Exodus 15:3).

SAVIOR David praised God by calling him "Savior" (2 Samuel 22:47). God had saved David from many dangers.

AWESOME ONE Asaph called God "the Awesome One" in Psalm 76:11 (NLT). Some translations of the Bible call God "the One to be feared" (NIV) or "him that ought to be feared" (KJV). When the Bible says that God is to be "feared," it usually means that we are to stand in awe of God and respect his awesome greatness and power.

LIGHT OF ISRAEL Isaiah calls God the "Light of Israel" (Isaiah 10:17). Just as light allows us to see where we are going, so God guides us and shows us the way to live. The Bible tells us that in heaven there will be no sun and moon, because God's glory will be the light (Revelation 21:23; 22:5).

ALPHA AND OMEGA "The Beginning and the End"
This is a name God calls himself (Revelation 21:6). "Alpha" is the first letter of the Greek alphabet. "Omega" is the last. The beings in heaven praise God night and day saying, "Holy, holy, holy is the Lord God Almighty, who was, and is, and is to come" (Revelation 4:8). God began all things, and he will end time as we know it. However, he gives us the gift of spending eternity with him.

Worship in the Bible: Who? How? Why?

Scripture

"Do not worship other gods. Rather, worship the Lord your God; it is he who will deliver you from the hand of all your enemies."   2 Kings 17:38, 39

Goal

Learn that worship is the response of God's people to who God is and what he has done.

INTRODUCTION *Introduction*

As the students arrive, give each one a pencil and a copy of the God Is handout (page 23). Ask them to use the clues on the page to help them fill in the blanks.

Answers: 1. Against evil; 2. Wise; 3. Everlasting; 4. Shepherd; 5. Our Maker; 6. Most High; 7. Excellent.

DISCOVERY RALLY

Gather the students together in a large group.

WHAT'S THE GOOD WORD?

Choose a student to read the Scripture for today.

THE CHALLENGE

Discuss the God Is handout, and let the students tell you the answers. Remind the students that worship is expressing our wonder and love for God, to God. Ask: **What are some reasons to worship God?** Then tell them that in their Discovery Centers today they will discover who worshiped in Bible times, how they worshiped, and why they worshiped.

PRAYER

DISCOVERY CENTERS

1. IDOL WORSHIP

MATERIALS
old magazines and newspapers, copies of the Idols handout (page 22), scissors, glue

DO: Bring old magazines and newspapers that are appropriate for the students to see. Give each student a copy of the Idols handout. Point out the idols that border the page. Say: **Idolatry is making something in your life more important to you than God.** Ask the students to find magazine and newspaper pictures of things that some people consider to be more important than God is. Tell the students to cut out some of these and glue them inside the outlined idol on their papers to make a montage. As they work, read Isaiah 44:12-20.

DISCUSS: All people, everywhere, in every time in history, have been tempted to worship or serve something other than God. How do some of the pictures you are cutting out act like idols? People may not bow down to them, but some people treat these things as more important than God. Whatever is most important to you is what you worship. You express your wonder and love for that thing. How can you tell if people worship sports or movies or just things? (They talk about these things more than they talk about God. They spend their money on these things, but don't give at church or to the poor.) **Whatever you spend most of your time thinking about, talking about, trying to get, or trying to do will probably be the most important thing in your life. If it is more important than God, it is an idol.**

2. RADIO REPORTERS

MATERIALS

copy of the Worshipers in the Bible handout (pages 24, 25), blank audio cassette tape, tape recorder

DO: Cut apart the character descriptions and the reporter's questions from the handout pages. Choose one student to be the radio reporter. Give that student the reporter's questions. Then give one character description to each remaining student. Tell the students that each of them will be playing the part of the character described on the slip of paper when the reporter interviews them. Give the students a few minutes to silently read the descriptions. Then tell the reporter to interview each character one by one, asking the questions on his slip of paper. As the reporter interviews each character, record their responses on the audio tape. Encourage the students to use character voices if they want to.

DISCUSS: Did these characters worship for the same reason? Did someone tell these people that they had to worship? What was their reason for worshiping? Did they all worship in the same way? How did they worship? Worship is expressing our wonder and love for God, to God. We have wonder and love for him because of who he is and what he has done for us. So who is God and what has he done for us? Worship is how we express our awe of God's greatness, our thanks for all he provides, and our love for him.

3. NEWSPAPER REPORTERS

MATERIALS

prepared index cards, newspaper, pencils, notebook paper, Bibles

Before the session, write each of the following Scripture references on a separate index card: Exodus 4:29-31; Exodus 12:12, 13, 17, 24-28; Exodus 34:4-8; 2 Chronicles 20:2, 3, 14-19; 2 Chronicles 29:18, 19, 27-30; Nehemiah 9:1-6; Matthew 2:9-11; Matthew 28:1-10; Acts 13:1-3; Revelation 19:4. On six other index cards, write with bold black letters: WHO?, WHAT?, WHEN?, WHERE?, HOW?, WHY? Then choose a few newspaper articles with headlines that would be appropriate for the students to see.

DO: Give each student a card, a pencil, a piece of paper, and a Bible (if they have not brought their own). On the table or wall, set out the six question cards where the students can see them clearly. Show the students the newspaper. Point out the headlines of the articles that you have chosen. Tell the students that when news reporters write articles for the newspaper, they try to answer the who, what, when, where, how, and why questions. Tell the students to write these six questions in a column down the left side of their papers, skipping a few lines between each question. Then ask the students to look up the Scripture written on the card, think about it as if they were newspaper reporters back then and they were going to write an article about it. Then have the students write a short answer to each question on their papers. Let them know that they may leave a question unanswered if they have to. Sometimes the Bible passage doesn't give us all the details. After they have answered all the questions they can, ask them to try to think of a headline that might fit that Bible passage if it were being written as an article.

DISCUSS: Remind the students that worship is expressing our wonder and love for God, to God. **What are you discovering about worship? What is it? Who can worship? Why do people worship? When? Where? How?**

DISCOVERERS' DEBRIEFING

If you have time to review, gather as a large group and discuss your young discoverers' findings. Ask the following questions:

- **What is the most interesting thing you discovered today?**
- **What did you learn today that you didn't know before?**
- **What is an idol?**
- **What are some kinds of idols that people have today?**
- **In Bible times, why did people worship God? How did they worship?**
- **Why should we worship God?**

Review the Scripture for today.

Pray, thanking God for teaching us about worship. Ask God to teach us more.

IDOLS THEN AND NOW

ancient Middle East idol

Egyptian god

Egyptian god

old idol of Crete

Buddhist idol

Hindu idol

GOD IS. . .

Fill in the blanks using the clues to discover who God is.

1. A_____ evil.

2. W____

3. E_____

4. S_____

5. O___ M_____

6. M_____ H____

7. E_____

Clues

1. If you are not *for* it, you are _____ it.
2. Very smart, understanding everything.
3. Lasting forever.
4. A person who takes care of sheep.
5. a. Belongs to us b. One who makes something
6. a. Opposite of least b. Opposite of low
7. Better than the best, great, super.

WORSHIPERS IN THE BIBLE

JOB (Job 38:1–42:3)

I had been asking questions about God. But then God talked to me and told me about all the wonderful things he had made. God asked me if I could make all those things. Then I realized how great and awesome God is. I told God, "I know that you can do all things." Telling God how great he is (and meaning it with all your heart) is one way to worship. I worshiped God because he is Elohim, the Mighty Maker.

SOLOMON (1 Kings 8:1-21, 54, 64-66)

God promised that a temple would be built for him while I was king of his people. When the workmen finished building this beautiful temple, I gathered the people together. God had kept his promise. I kneeled with my hands out toward heaven. I worshiped God, praying out loud. I said, "O Lord, . . . there is no God like you in heaven above or on earth below—you who keep your covenant of love" (1 Kings 8:23).

NOAH (Genesis 6–8)

God told me to build a large boat to hold my family and some of every kind of animal. When we were all in the boat, the rains came. It kept raining for forty days and nights. Even when the rain stopped, the water stayed high for a long time. At last the water went down and we all came out of the ark. Then I built an altar and gave sacrifices to God on the altar. I worshiped God, because he had kept us safe.

MARY (Luke 1:39-56)

An angel named Gabriel came to me and told me that I would be the mother of God's Son. I went to see my relative Elizabeth, an older woman. An angel had told her husband that they, too, would have a special baby. In fact, when I got to Elizabeth's house, she felt her baby jump inside her. She knew that I would have a baby, God's Son. I was so excited that I worshiped God right then and there. I praised him with a song: "God has done mighty deeds. He has filled the hungry with good things. He has remembered mercy!"

HEZEKIAH (Isaiah 38)

I was sick in bed. Isaiah the prophet came and told me that I would not live much longer. But I prayed, and God healed me. I worshiped by writing my feelings: "What can I say? [God] has spoken to me, and he himself has done this. . . . You restored me to health and let me live. . . . We will sing with stringed instruments all the days of our lives in the temple of the Lord" (Isaiah 38:15-20).

A LEPER (Luke 17:11-19)

I had leprosy, a terrible skin disease. I had to live outside the towns, away from family and friends. The only friends I had were other lepers like me. But one day we saw Jesus and called to him. He told us to go show ourselves to the priest. As we went, we realized we were healed! Right away, I ran back to Jesus and threw myself down at his feet. I thanked him with all my heart, because I was well.

PAUL (Acts 9:1-31)

I believed in God, but I didn't believe in Jesus. In fact, I captured Christians and put them in jail. One day I was on the way to arrest some Christians. A bright light shone on me. Jesus spoke to me. Then I knew that Jesus was real. But I was blind. I spent three days worshiping, praying to God, not eating or drinking. Then God sent a man to heal me so that I could see again. I have followed Jesus ever since.

MARY (MARTHA'S SISTER) (John 12:1-8)

My sister Martha, my brother Lazarus, and I gave a dinner party for Jesus. Martha served food. My brother Lazarus sat at the table with Jesus. I wanted to honor Jesus, too. So I took some expensive perfume and poured it on Jesus' feet. Then I wiped his feet with my long hair. I was worshiping Jesus, showing him that he was more important than even the most expensive perfume.

DANIEL (Daniel 2)

I served King Nebuchadnezzar in Babylon. One night the king had a strange dream. He wanted the wise men to tell him the dream and its meaning. Of course they couldn't tell him what he dreamed. Only the king knew that. The king was angry. He was going to kill all the wise men. That included me and my friends. So I prayed to God, and he told me the dream and its meaning. I worshiped God. I said, "Praise be to the name of God for ever and ever. . . . He reveals deep and hidden things. . . . I thank and praise you, O God of my fathers" (Daniel 2:20-23).

HANNAH (1 Samuel 1, 2)

Year after year my husband and I went to Shiloh to worship God at the worship tent there. But I was always sad, because I had no children. Then one year at the worship tent, I prayed for a baby. The old priest saw my mouth moving with my silent prayer, and he thought I was drunk. But I told him I had been pouring out my heart to God. The priest blessed me, and I went home. Then I found out that God had blessed me, too. He gave me the baby I had asked for. I was overjoyed, and I was thankful. I worshiped God and prayed, "There is no one holy like the Lord; there is no one besides you; there is no Rock like our God" (1 Samuel 2:2).

Reporter's Questions	What is your name?	Why did you worship God?
	Did anyone else worship with you?	How did you worship?

Life as Worship

scripture

"Offer your lives as a living sacrifice to [God]. Your offering must be only for God and pleasing to him. This is the spiritual way for you to worship. " Romans 12:1, 2, ICB

Goal

Learn that the way we live shows who or what we worship. Learn that as God's children, our lives are worship, because we do all things, large or small, to honor and glorify him.

INTRODUCTION

As students arrive, seat them in a circle, adding more students to the circle as they arrive. Ask each student to think of an adjective (describing word) that starts with the same sound as the beginning letter of his name. For example, Silly Samuel, Magnificent Maria, Excellent Eric. Choose one student in the circle to start the game. This student says his name with its describing word. The next student says the first student's name with an adjective and then her own name with an adjective. The third student says the previous two students' names with adjectives and then his own name with an adjective. Continue this way, adding each student's name as the game goes around the circle. Help those who have difficulty remembering as well as those who come in during the game.

DISCOVERY RALLY

Gather the students together in a large group.

WHAT'S THE GOOD WORD?

Choose a student to read the Scripture for today.

THE CHALLENGE

Ask: **Did the descriptive word you chose in the introductory activity really describe yourself? Was it the only word that you could have chosen?** Ask a student to read Psalm 139:1-18. **How much does God know about you? God made you just the way you are and is pleased with the way you are made. When we give our lives to God, everything we do becomes worship, an expression of our honor for God.** Tell the students that they will learn why in their Discovery Centers today.

PRAYER

DISCOVERY CENTERS

1. THE GIFT BOX

DO: Set the index cards in stacks on the table along with pencils or markers. Ask the students to write or draw an object or scene that shows something about their lives. (For example, they can draw a soccer ball or write "soccer" if soccer is part of "who they are." You can give them suggestions: your favorite food, music lessons, your room, your hobby, friends, school, or a collection of something.) When they have done a few cards, ask the students to place their cards in their boxes and gift wrap them. This represents the gift of their lives given to God.

MATERIALS
index cards, pencils or markers, small boxes (large enough to hold index cards) or envelopes, wrapping paper, scissors, tape, bows

DISCUSS: **What does it mean to give your life to God? How can we give our lives to God?** Read Colossians 3:23, 24; 1 Corinthians 10:31; 1 Corinthians 3:16. **What part of our lives belongs to God?** (All of it.) **How can cleaning our bedrooms be worship? How can doing homework be worship? What are some of the**

cards you are placing in your boxes? For example, how can music lessons be worship? When we have given our lives to God, we do everything with a respectful, loving attitude toward him. We live in God's presence every moment. So everything we do should honor him. We work and play with God in mind, knowing his Spirit lives in us.

2. OUR SACRIFICE

MATERIALS
paper, pencils or pens

DO: Give each student a piece of paper and a pencil or pen. Ask the students to write the letters of the word *sacrifice* in a column down the left hand side of the paper. Ask the students to use each letter in the word *sacrifice* to begin another word, a word of something in their lives that is not as important as God. For example: shopping, apples, camp, reading, ice cream, friends, internet, candy, e-mail.

DISCUSS: What is a sacrifice? In Bible times, God's people would give a sacrifice to God—something of value like a sheep or bull or the first of their crops. This showed that they valued God above everything else. It was expressing their love for God, to God. What do missionaries sacrifice to teach others about Jesus? God may not ask us to give up the things we listed, but he does ask us to never put them first in our lives. A worshipful attitude toward God (putting God first) shows in us no matter what we do. Ask the students about some of the things they've listed: **How would an attitude of worship (putting God first) show up when we are shopping? How would an attitude of worship show up when we are with friends? How would an attitude of worship show up when we are surfing the internet?**

3. AN ALTAR PAPERWEIGHT

MATERIALS
bag of small decorative rocks, glue,
paper plates, picture of a stone altar

DO: Give each student at least ten rocks and a paper plate. Show students the picture of the altar. (You can find this in a Bible dictionary, or a student's Bible that has pictures it). Ask the students to glue the ten rocks together to build a small altar on the paper plate.

DISCUSS: What is an altar? It used to be a special place to worship. It was a place to offer a gift to God, a sacrifice. In Bible times, people offered the meat of animals, grain, fruit, wine, and incense on altars. The oldest kinds of altars from Bible times were made of mud bricks. Sometimes they were just mounds of dirt. But most of the altars in the time before Solomon were built of stone.

Read Romans 12:1, 2, the Scripture for today. **What do you think that Scripture means? How can our lives be "living sacrifices"?** It may be easier to understand if we say "living gifts." **How can we be "living gifts" for God?** Being a living sacrifice means choosing to honor or worship God in all we do and with all we have, expressing our wonder and love of God, to God.

DISCOVERERS' DEBRIEFING

If you have time to review, gather as a large group and discuss your young discoverers' findings. Ask the following questions:
- What is the most interesting thing you discovered today?
- What did you learn today that you didn't know before?
- What part of our lives does God want us to give him?
- What does it mean for us to be a living sacrifice?
- How do we do everything "as working for the Lord"?
- What is an attitude of worship?

Review the Scripture for today.

Pray, telling God that we give ourselves to him as living sacrifices. Tell him that we plan to honor him in all we do.

When David Worshiped

scripture

"*Praise the Lord for the glory of his name. Worship the Lord because he is holy.*"   Psalm 29:2, ICB

Goal

Learn that we can worship no matter how we feel, because worship is simply putting God on the throne in our hearts.

INTRODUCTION

As the students arrive, give each of them a copy of the Around the Heart handout (page 35). Starting at the arrow, they will go around the heart clockwise, writing every other letter in the blanks below the heart. They will have to go around the heart twice.

Answer: "Greater love has no one than this, that he lay down his life for his friends."

DISCOVERY RALLY

Gather the students together in a large group.

WHAT'S THE GOOD WORD?

Choose a student to read the Scripture for today.

THE CHALLENGE

Ask: **What does the word** *holy* **mean?** (It means different and set apart.) **What makes God different and set apart from all other beings? Some people worship false gods. What makes our God different from other people's gods?** Ask different students to read the following verses to answer that question:

- Deuteronomy 3:23-29
- Deuteronomy 4:1-8 (especially verse 7)
- 2 Chronicles 6:14
- 2 Chronicles 14:11
- Psalm 25:14
- Psalm 66:5
- Isaiah 64:4, 5
- 1 John 4:8 (We never find the teaching "God is love" in any other religion.)

David worshiped God because God is holy: different and set apart. David expressed his wonder and love of God, to God. Tell the students that in their Discovery Centers today they will learn more about worshiping God no matter how we feel, because worship is simply putting God "on the throne in our hearts."

PRAYER

DISCOVERY CENTERS

1. PRAISE WINDOWS

DO: Give each student a copy of the Praise Window handout. Point out the definitions that are written in each of the seven sections of the window. Tell the students that you will tell them a Hebrew word for praise that goes with each definition. Ask the students to use a dark crayon to write each Hebrew word in its proper section. As you tell the students the words, spell the words for them.

> *Hallal* (to rave, talk with extreme excitement)
>
> *Yadah* (to lift the hands)
>
> *Barak* (to kneel and declare God as the source of power)
>
> *Tehillah* (to sing praise spontaneously)
>
> *Zamar* (to touch the strings, play stringed music)
>
> *To'dah* (to thank and praise God for what he is going to do)
>
> *Shabach* (to shout)

After the students have written these words in each section, ask them to color each section a different color. Then give each student a cotton ball. Have each student put baby oil on his cotton ball and rub it over the window area of the page. (This makes the window area translucent.) Allow the students to take these home and hang them in their windows to let the light shine through them.

DISCUSS: When we read the word *praise* in our Bibles, it could mean any of these words in Hebrew. When David and others wrote the psalms, they used these words to praise God. Read Psalm 22:1-26. How do you think David felt when he wrote this psalm? In verses 22, 23, and 26, he used the word *hallal*. He wrote about raving, or talking excitedly, about God. Why? Discuss the other psalms written in the praise window. Ask the students how David felt when he wrote each psalm. Ask them what word he used to express praise in each psalm. The only psalm in the praise window that was not written by David is the one in the *to'dah* window. A man named Asaph wrote that psalm. These psalms show us that we can worship no matter how we feel, because worship is simply putting God on the "throne in our hearts." It is expressing our love of God to God.

MATERIALS

copies of the Praise Window handout (page 36), crayons, cotton balls, baby oil

2. GUESS HOW I FEEL?

Before the session, write the name of several different emotions on different index cards, one emotion per card. (Suggestions: happy, sad, bored, excited, angry, surprised, shy, scared, loving, confused, worried, awed, proud.)

MATERIALS
prepared index cards

DO: Hold the emotion cards in your hand as if you were holding a hand of playing cards (so you see the words on the cards, but the students see only the backs of the cards). Choose one student to go first. Have that student draw a card and silently read the emotion written on it. Then instruct that student to act out the emotion. Have the other students try to guess what emotion the student is portraying. Let each student take a turn.

DISCUSS: Has there ever been a time when you didn't feel like praising God and singing with excitement and joy? David didn't worship because he felt a certain emotion. He worshiped because of who God is: different and special. Worship is simply making God the most important one in our lives, telling him so, and living like it. David loved God when he was happy, sad, angry, afraid, or excited. So he expressed that wonder and love of God no matter how he felt. To read some of the emotions expressed in David's worship, turn to the following psalms.

Psalm 2:1-5 (puzzled)
Psalm 6:6, 7 (sad)
Psalm 8 (awed)
Psalm 9:1-11 (joyful)
Psalm 13 (lonely)
Psalm 18 (thankful)
Psalm 23 (peaceful)
Psalm 31 (fearful)
Psalm 38 (guilty)
Psalm 51 (sorrowful, repentant)

3. PSALM 100

MATERIALS
Bibles, colored pencils and stencil sheets of alphabet letters, lined noteboook paper

DO: Give each student a sheet of paper and a set of stencils. Ask the students to turn to Psalm 100 in a Bible. Then tell them to use the stencils to write verse 1 and verse 4 on their papers with colored pencils. If you have extra time, let them design a border for the page.

DISCUSS: This psalm talks about five things we do in worship. Can you find these five things? (These five things are not just in verses 1 and 4, so the students will have to read all five verses to find them. They are shouting for joy, serving the Lord, singing, giving thanks, and praising his name. NOTE: While all five things are found in the NIV and other versions, only the NAS and ICB use all five words exactly as listed in this activity.) Two of these things tell the feeling of the person doing them. What are these two? (Shouting for joy and giving thanks.) The other three don't tell the feeling of the person doing them. Can these three be done no matter how we feel? Explain.

DISCOVERERS' DEBRIEFING

If you have time to review, gather as a large group and discuss your young discoverers' findings. Ask the following questions:

- What is the most interesting thing you discovered today?
- What did you learn today that you didn't know before?
- What are some different Hebrew words for praise?
- What do some of these words mean?
- If we are not feeling joyful, does that mean we can't worship? Explain.
- What are some emotions that David expressed in worship?

If you were not able to read some or all of David's emotions expressed in the psalms, do that now.

Review the Scripture for today.

Pray, thanking God that we can worship no matter how we feel. Tell God that we place him on the throne in our hearts.

AROUND THE HEART

Start at the starting arrow and go around the heart twice, writing every other letter in the blanks below. You will find what true love is, and you will finish this verse:

"Greater love has no one than this, . . .

Start

t l s s d i n h
i e
h n
f i
a w
e o
t r
f o
h f
o d
e s
r i
l a
h y

"

‗ ‗ ‗ ‗ ‗ ‗ ‗ ‗ ‗ ‗ ‗

‗ ‗ ‗ ‗ ‗ ‗ ‗ ‗

‗ ‗ ‗ ‗ ‗ ‗ ‗ ‗ ‗ ‗ ." John 15:13

Who did this for you?

John wrote, "We love because he first loved us" (1 John 4:19).

PRAISE WINDOW

Psalm 22, 23, 26
to rave; talk with excitement

Psalm 9:1, 2
to lift the hands

Psalm 16:7
to kneel and declare God
as the source of power

Psalm 42:4
to thank and praise God for what he is going to do

Psalm 34:1
to sing praise
spontaneously

Psalm 7:17
to play stringed music

Psalm 145:1-3
to shout

Write Your Own Psalm

Scripture

"Sing to the Lord a new song; sing to the Lord, all the earth." Psalm 96:1

Goal

Practice worshiping by writing our own psalms.

INTRODUCTION

As the students arrive, give each student a copy of the The Greatest Commandment handout (page 41). Challenge the students to figure out the verse using the code.

Answer: "Love the Lord your God with all your heart and with all your soul and with all your mind."

DISCOVERY RALLY

Gather the students together in a large group.

WHAT'S THE GOOD WORD?

Choose a student to read the Scripture for today.

THE CHALLENGE

Ask: **What did the coded verse say? How do we love the Lord with all our heart, soul, and mind?** One preschool girl described worship in this way: "Worship is . . ." and then she blew a kiss up toward God in heaven. **God first loved us. Worship is our way of loving God back.** Tell the students that today they will stay in the same Discovery Centers for the length of two group times, then they will gather in a large group. Tell them that they will be writing their own psalms and worshiping with them.

PRAYER

DISCOVERY GROUPS

All three Discovery Centers will do this activity first:

1. PSALM 103

MATERIALS
copies of the Psalm 103 handout
(page 42)

DO: Give each student a copy of the psalm hand-out. Ask the students to read the first two verses. **To whom is David talking? If you were writing a psalm, you could write to yourself. But even David did not write all psalms to himself. To whom could you write? You could write your psalm to others.** (You can see how this was done in Psalm 100.) **Or you could write your psalm to God. This is the purest form of worship: talking directly to God.** (You can see how David did this in Psalm 101.)

Now ask the students to read verses 3 through 7. **What do these verses tell us?** (They tell us what God has done.) Ask the students to read verses 8 through 10. **What are these verses telling us?** (They describe God, telling us who God is and what he's like.) Ask the students to read verses 11 through 19. **What are these verses talking about?** (They are describing God's love and his relationship with us.) Ask the students to read verses 20 through 22. **To whom are these verses addressed? Why do you think David wrote this to the angels and heavenly hosts?** Now ask the students to read verse 5 again. **What does this mean? Sometimes writers of songs and poetry say "this" is like "that." David says his youth (or energy, feeling young) is made new like what?** (Like the eagle's energy.) **This is a word picture. It's like painting with words. Does this word picture make David's thoughts clear to you?** Ask the students to read verses 15 and 16. **This is a word picture, too. What is David trying to paint with these words?**

All three Discovery Centers will do this activity second:

2. WRITING OUR OWN PSALMS

MATERIALS
notebook paper, pencils

DO: Give each student paper and a pencil. You may let the students work in pairs if you think it would be easier for them.
Ask them not to put a title on their psalm yet. Tell them to decide whether they will write this psalm to themselves, to someone else, or to God. Then ask the students to write a line of praise for God, addressed to the one they decided to write this psalm to. (See the comments on Psalm 103:1, 2 in the Discovery Center #1.)

Ask the students to write four lines, each line telling something that God has done. (If this is addressed to God, it will say, "You have . . ." If this is addressed to someone else or to themselves, it will say, "He has . . .") Remind them that they can write a word picture if they want: "He has warmed me like a fire on a winter day. He has made my heart feel as clean as a freshly washed bed sheet."

Now ask the students to write four lines describing God. (If this is addressed to God, it will say, "You are . . ." If this is addressed to someone else or to themselves, it will say, "He is . . ." Remind them that they can write a word picture if they want: He is kinder than the kindest mother. He is stronger than a hurricane.)

Ask the students to write two lines about God's relationship with people. (He loves the people he has made. He guides us. He helps us. He watches over us.)

Last of all, ask the students to write a line of praise addressed to something or some-one besides the one to whom they are writing the psalm. (See Psalm 103:20-22 discussed in Discovery Center #1.) Then instruct them to finish with the same line of praise with which they began the psalm. Ask each student to sign his name at the bottom of his psalm and put a title at the top. (The title can incorporate the student's name if she wants, as in "Christen's Psalm.")

3. WORSHIPING WITH OUR OWN PSALMS

Before the session, recruit someone who can play guitar, keyboard, or other instrument to join you and quietly play background music as the students read their psalms aloud to the Lord. Ask all the groups to come together to form one large group. You may give each student the option of reading her own psalm, choosing another student to read it, or asking you to read it. Worship the Lord together. If there are some funny moments, feel free to laugh together and then continue on.

MATERIALS

psalms written in Discovery Center #2, musical accompanist

DISCOVERERS' DEBRIEFING

If you have time, review the findings for today. Ask the following questions:
- **What is the most interesting thing you discovered today?**
- **What did you learn today that you didn't know before?**
- **If you want to write your own psalms, how can you go about it?**

Encourage the students to write more psalms on their own as they worship God. Tell them that the one they wrote today is only one kind of psalm. They can express any feeling to God as they worship with psalms.

Review the Scripture for today.

Pray, thanking God for inviting us to come to him in worship. Thank God for giving each one of us the ability to worship him with psalms.

The Greatest Commandment

Jesus said that the first and greatest commandment is:

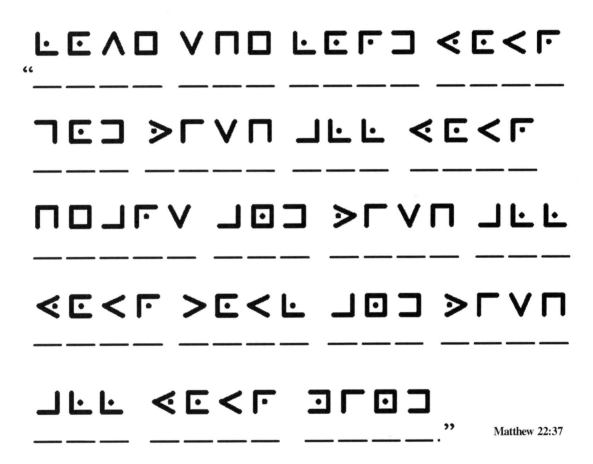

" _____ _____ _____ _____ _____ _____

_____ _____ _____ _____

_____ _____ _____ _____

_____ _____ _____ _____

_____ _____ _____ . "

Matthew 22:37

Use this code to solve the puzzle:

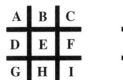

PSALM 103
of David

1 Praise the Lord, O my soul;
   all my inmost being, praise his holy name.

2 Praise the Lord, O my soul,
   and forget not all his benefits—

3 who forgives all your sins
   and heals all your diseases,

4 who redeems your life from the pit
   and crowns you with love and compassion,

5 who satisfies your desires with good things
   so that your youth is renewed like the eagle's.

6 The Lord works righteousness
   and justice for all the oppressed.

7 He made known his ways to Moses,
   his deeds to the people of Israel:

8 The Lord is compassionate and gracious,
   slow to anger, abounding in love.

9 He will not always accuse,
   nor will he harbor his anger forever;

10 he does not treat us as our sins deserve
   or repay us according to our iniquities.

11 For as high as the heavens are above the earth,
   so great is his love for those who fear him;

12 as far as the east is from the west,
   so far has he removed our transgressions from us.

13 As a father has compassion on his children,
   so the Lord has compassion on those who fear
   him;

14 for he knows how we are formed,
   he remembers that we are dust.

15 As for man, his days are like grass,
   he flourishes like a flower of the field;

16 the wind blows over it and it is gone,
   and its place remembers it no more.

17 But from everlasting to everlasting
   the Lord's love is with those who fear him,
   and his righteousness with their children's
   children—

18 with those who keep his covenant
   and remember to obey his precepts.

19 The Lord has established his throne in heaven,
   and his kingdom rules over all.

20 Praise the Lord, you his angels,
   you mighty ones who do his bidding,
   who obey his word.

21 Praise the Lord, all his heavenly hosts,
   you his servants who do his will.

22 Praise the Lord, all his works
   everywhere in his dominion.
   Praise the Lord, O my soul.

Quiet, Thoughtful Worship

Scripture

"Be still, and know that I am God."   Psalm 46:10

Goal

Learn that sometimes worship is simply sitting and thinking about God, wondering about him, and asking him questions about himself.

INTRODUCTION

As the students arrive, give each one a pencil and the Puzzle Page handout (page 49). Ask them to copy exactly what they see from the numbered boxes at the top of the page into the boxes with the matching numbers at the bottom of the page.

DISCOVERY RALLY

Gather the students together in a large group.

WHAT'S THE GOOD WORD?

Choose a student to read the Scripture for today.

THE CHALLENGE

Refer to the Scripture on the Puzzle Page handout that the students have just completed: "Give me an undivided heart" (Psalm 86:11). Ask: **What is an undivided heart? What did you find at the center of the heart when you worked out the puzzle?** (An undivided heart is a heart that puts God first before anything else. It is a heart that worships God.) **In past lessons you've learned that worship is expressing our wonder and love for God to God. It is living in a way that**

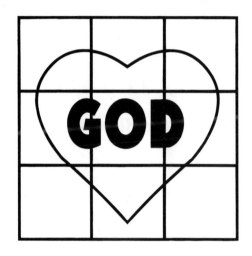

shows that God is first in our lives. **You've learned that worship is an attitude of respect toward God. Worship can be praise. Can you remember some of the Hebrew words for praise?** (*Hallal,* "raving"; *yadah,* "lifting hands"; *barak,* "kneeling"; *tehillah,* "spontaneous singing"; *zamar,* "with instruments"; *to'dah,* "thanks for what God's going to do"; and *shabach,* "shouting.") **These words describe worship as loud and active. But worship can also be quiet and thoughtful.** Tell the students that today in their Discovery Centers, they will learn about quiet, thoughtful worship.

PRAYER

DISCOVERY CENTERS

1. SEEING GOD IN HIS CREATION

MATERIALS
magnifying glass (or several if you have access to more than one), bouquet containing several different kinds of flowers

Before the session, purchase a bouquet of flowers. These are usually fairly inexpensive at supermarkets that have floral departments. If you want to allow each student to take a flower home at the end of the day, you may need more than one bouquet to get one flower per student.

DO: If you are able, do this activity outdoors in a natural setting. Show the students the bouquet. Ask them to look carefully at the flowers and tell you some of the differences in them. Pass the individual flowers around the group and let the students take turns looking at the flowers and leaves and smelling the flowers.

DISCUSS: Do you see anything especially interesting as you look closely at your flowers? Notice the veins in the leaves, the different shapes of leaves and petals, the scents, the differences in color. What do all of these things tell you about God? Can you remember what Jesus said about flowers? (God takes care of flowers, so we know God will take care of us—Matthew 6:28-30.)

Next, ask a student to read Romans 1:20. Ask a student to read Psalm 19:1-4. **What do these verses tell us about the world God made? One way to worship is to quietly think about God and to wonder about him. Sometimes we call this "meditating on God." We can also meditate on God's Word. For example, we can think about what Jesus said about God taking care of flowers.**

Ask the students: **What are some other things that we call nature?** After they have given some examples of nature, ask them to close their eyes and be silent and think about God's creation, the things we call nature. After a few minutes, ask the students to continue thinking about God and to talk to God silently, telling him what most impresses them about his creation. This is quiet worship.

2. THINK!

Before the session, cut a star shape out of felt. The star should be about 1 to 1 1/2 inches across, small enough for a student to hold in his fist.

MATERIALS
felt, scissors

DO: Divide the students into two groups. You need three or more students in each group. Choose a leader for each group. The groups should be seated across the table from each other. Give the felt star to the leader in group 1. With hands beneath the table, group 1 begins passing the star back and forth to each other. The leader in group 1 gets to call "Think!" at any point. When she calls "Think!" the members of group 1 must pull their fists above the table and rest their elbows on the table with fists under their chins as if thinking. Group 2 takes a moment to talk about who they think has the star. Then the leader of group 2 calls out the names of the students in group 1 whom he believes do not have the star. As each student's name is called, that student must open his hands to show whether he has the star. If one of the students whose name is called does have the star, then group 1 gets to pass the star for another round of play. If group 2 is correct, and the last name called has the star, then group 2 gets to pass the star and group 1 must call "Think!"

DISCUSS: After each group has had a chance to pass the star, stop the game and talk for a few minutes about stars. **Astronomers tell us that there are more than 200 billion stars. That means that if each person in the world were to count different stars, each person would have to count over 50 billion stars without counting the same star twice! What is our nearest star?** (It's the sun.) **It's 100 times as large as our earth, but it's only a medium-sized star. Can you think of a place in the Bible that talks about stars?** (Creation; God's promise to Abraham in Genesis 15:5 and 22:17; Joseph's dream about the stars bowing down; the wise men traveling to see baby Jesus.) **Close your eyes for a minute and think about the stars. Think about God's greatness and wisdom as the Creator of the stars.** While the students have their eyes closed, read Psalm 147:4 and then Psalm 8:1-4. Tell the students that as they quietly think about God's greatness, they can silently thank him for creating space. They can ask God how he can know the names of all those stars. This silent thinking about God is a part of quiet worship.

If you have time: Play "Think!" again.

3. TINY ATOMS, AWESOME GOD

MATERIALS
copies of Tiny Atoms, Awesome God
(page 50), box of table salt, tennis
ball, sheet of paper

DO: Ask the students what an atom is. It is one of the smallest parts of what everything is made of. Show one copy of the handout to the group. Tell them that this diagram is huge compared to the size of a real atom. A real atom is too small to be seen under most microscopes. Point out the nucleus (center) of the atom and the electrons that circle around the atom like the moon circles around the earth. Tell the students that an atom is made of mostly empty space between each of the parts.

Pour a bit of salt into each student's hand. Ask the students to look at a single grain of salt. Tell them these two amazing facts:

- Each of these grains of salt contains many, many atoms. If each of the atoms in the piece of salt was as large as the grain of salt, the grain of salt would have to be over six miles wide!
- If you removed all the space from the atoms in your body, you would be no bigger than that grain of salt!

Show the students a tennis ball. Ask: **How many of you have ever been to a football game? Picture a football stadium. If we could make one atom grow large enough to fill a football stadium, the nucleus (center) would be the size of this tennis ball at the 50-yard line (in the center of the field) and the electrons circling around it would be tiny dots at the goal lines.**

Give the students the copy of the handout. Ask them to look at the edge of the paper to see how thin the paper is. Tell the students that atoms are so small that 1 million hydrogen atoms could line up side by side and still not be as thick as this sheet of paper.

DISCUSS: Close your eyes and think about God, the Creator of the atoms. God created the sun, moon and stars, huge mountains, and tall trees out of tiny atoms that we can't even see. Not even the smartest scientists have figured out all there is to know about huge outer space or small "inner space" (the atoms which are the building blocks of us and everything around us). Read Job 38 aloud. Then ask the students to be silent and to think and wonder about God and what he created. Suggest that they silently thank him for his creation. After a few minutes, tell the students that this silent thinking and wondering about God is one way to worship.

The students can take home the diagram of the atom.

DISCOVERERS' DEBRIEFING

If you have time to review, gather as a large group and discuss your young discoverers' findings. Ask the following questions:

- What is the most interesting thing you discovered today?
- What did you learn today that you didn't know before?
- How can we worship quietly?
- Do we have to be thinking about nature or atoms to worship quietly?
- How can we worship quietly by meditating on God's Word?

Review the Scripture for today.

Pray, expressing awe to God for who he is and what he has done.

PUZZLE PAGE

David said to God, "Give me an undivided heart" (Psalm 86:11). What did David want to center his whole heart on? To find the answer, copy exactly what you see from the numbered boxes in the top section of this page into the matching numbered boxes below.

1.	2.	3.
4.	5.	6.
7.	8.	9.

WORSHIP The foundation for loving God

TINY ATOMS, AWESOME GOD

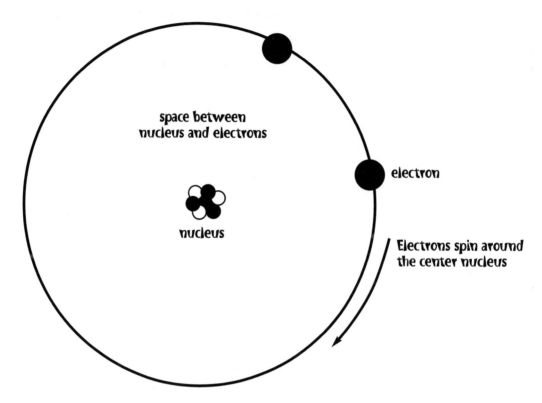

space between
nucleus and electrons

electron

nucleus

Electrons spin around
the center nucleus

Atomic Facts

✔ An atom is too small to be seen under most microscopes, yet it is made mostly of empty space
between each of the parts.

✔ A grain of salt contains many, many atoms. If each of the atoms in the piece of salt was as
large as the grain of salt itself, the grain of salt would have to be over six miles wide!

✔ If you removed all the space from the atoms in your body, you would be no bigger than a
grain of salt!

✔ If we could make one atom grow large enough to fill a football stadium, the nucleus (center)
would be the size of a tennis ball at the 50-yard line and the electrons circling around it
would be tiny dots at the goal lines.

✔ 1 million hydrogen atoms could line up side by side and still not be as thick as this sheet of
paper.

Isn't the Creator awesome?!!

Worshiping With Music

Scripture

"Praise him with the sounding of the trumpet, praise him with the harp and lyre, praise him with tambourine and dancing, praise him with the strings and flute, praise him with the clash of cymbals, praise him with resounding cymbals. Let everything that has breath praise the Lord."   Psalm 150:3-6

Goal

Learn that making music is one way to worship God.

INTRODUCTION

As the students arrive, direct them to join together in a large group. This game can be joined at any time as students continue to arrive. Choose one student to whistle or hum the first three notes of a tune that the others should know. The other students try to guess what the tune is. If no one guesses, the student whistles or hums again, adding three more notes. The others try to guess again. Notes are added, three at a time, until someone guesses the tune. The student who guesses correctly gets to be the new whistler. If no one guesses, the whistler tells what the tune was and chooses a new whistler.

DISCOVERY RALLY

Gather the students together in a large group.

WHAT'S THE GOOD WORD?

Choose a student to read the Scripture for today.

THE CHALLENGE

Ask: **Why would God want us to worship with music? What makes the difference between a worship song and any other song? What do we call music that has no singing?** (It's instrumental music.) **Why do you think it's called instrumental?** (Because it uses only instruments.) **Can instrumental music be worship music? Why or why not?** Tell the students that in their Discovery Centers today, they will learn more about worshiping with music.

PRAYER

DISCOVERY CENTERS

1. INSTRUMENTAL RIDDLES

If you play an instrument that is portable, bring it to demonstrate how to play it to the students. If you don't play an instrument, but you know someone who does, ask him to visit your class today and bring the instrument to play for the students.

MATERIALS

musical instrument and someone to play it, copies of the Instrumental Riddles handout (page 56), pencils

DO: Distribute the Instrumental Riddles handout. First, ask the students to read the riddle on the left-hand side of the page and then draw a line from the riddle to the picture on the right-hand side that shows the musical instrument that was used in Bible times. Then show the students the instrument you brought, or introduce the visitor who has brought an instrument. Tell the students how to play the instrument, then show the students how. If you feel comfortable doing so, let the students try playing the instrument.

DISCUSS: Do any of you play instruments? What instrument do you play? How have you learned (or are learning) to play? Did you know that King David chose people to sing and play worship music? Ask a student to read 1 Chronicles 25:1, 6-8. These verses tell us that there were teachers and students. They learned and practiced making music solely for the purpose of worship.

2. MELODY-MAKERS AND TAMBOURINES

MATERIALS
small, inexpensive combs, white tissue paper, scissors, large disposable Styrofoam picnic plates, duct tape, crepe paper streamers of different colors cut into 2-foot lengths

DO: For the melody-maker, give each student a comb. Ask the students to cut out a square of tissue paper that is as long as the comb and about twice as wide. To play the melody-maker, instruct the students to fold the tissue paper around the comb, with the teeth of the comb at the fold. Then have them place their lips, mouth slightly open, against the fold of the tissue paper and then blow gently and hum. (They should hear a buzzing melody.)

For the tambourine, give each student four streamers, a plate, and duct tape. Tell the students to use small strips of duct tape to tape one end of each streamer along one edge of the circular plate as shown. Then have the students hold the other edge with one hand and tap the bottom of the plate against the palm of the other hand. Ask the students to take turns tapping out a simple rhythm that the others can follow. Then try singing some of the worship songs you and your students know using the tambourine and the melody-makers that they have made.

DISCUSS: Think about the beginning of the world. Imagine that you are Adam and that you have just been created. There were no instruments. What would Adam have heard that would have sounded like music? (Birds, animal calls, wind, brooks and rivers.) **How could Adam have made music?** (He could have made an instrument; he could have sung.) Ask a student to read Genesis 4:21. **The flute is one of the first instruments in the world.** Ask a student to read the heading of Psalm 5 in an NIV Bible: "For the director of music. For flutes. A psalm of David." **It looks as though David wanted this song to be accompanied by flutes. What**

instruments do we use today to worship God or to express our wonder and love for him to him? Which instrument is your favorite?

3. PRAISE CHAIRS

Before the session, make a paper sign that says "Praise Chair." Then write one of the following Scripture references on each of ten index cards:

MATERIALS

paper, marker, prepared index cards, tape, Bible, instrument (if you play one) or a worship audio cassette or CD and player

Psalm 32:7	Psalm 65:8
Psalm 77:6	Psalm 96:1-4
Psalm 98:1	Psalm 100:2
Psalm 107:21, 22	Psalm 126:1, 2
Psalm 126:6	Psalm 138:1, 2

DO: Place enough chairs in a circle so that there is one for each student. On the back of one chair, tape the "Praise Chair" sign. Under the praise chair, stack the index cards, facedown. Lay the Bible on the floor in the center of the circle, opened to Psalms. Play a lively worship song (on your own instrument or with audio cassette or CD). Ask the students to walk around the circle as you play the song. Instruct the students to sit in the chair closest to them when the music stops. Stop the music at random. The student who sits in the "Praise Chair" takes the top card from the stack under the chair. She then turns to that psalm in the Bible and reads the verse. Ask the students why the writer of this psalm wanted to worship, or what kind of song this Scripture tells us about.

DISCUSS: Why do we worship when we come together? Why would God want people to worship with instruments? God wants us to worship him with all that we have and do. He wants to be at the center of our hearts. Our music comes from our hearts and expresses our feelings. God is interested in our feelings and wants us to give our hearts to him. Music is one way to do this. And that's worship.

DISCOVERERS' DEBRIEFING

If you have time to review, gather as a large group and discuss your young discoverers' findings. Ask the following questions:

- What is the most interesting thing you discovered today?
- What did you learn today that you didn't know before?
- What were some of the instruments people used in Bible times?
- Who led and accompanied worship in King David's time?
- Why do we worship when we come together?
- Why would God want people to worship with instruments?
- Can we worship in song without instruments? Why or why not?
- Can we worship with songs that have instruments but no voices? Why or why not?

Review the Scripture for today.

Pray, thanking God for music, for instruments, and for our own voices. Ask God to help us worship him in our music as well as in everything else we do.

INSTRUMENTAL RIDDLES

Draw a line from the riddle to the instrument it describes.

My sound warned people of danger, announced when the moon was new, and was used as a signal. You would play me by blowing. I come from part of an animal.

I was a very popular instrument. I was often used with singers. Sometimes I was made with costly woods and metals. You would play me by holding me in your arms and plucking or strumming. David wrote many songs with me.

I was a favorite instrument of the Egyptians. I was also played by plucking or strumming. And I was sometimes made with costly woods and metals. But I was large. You could not hold me in your arms.

I was made of reeds or metal or ivory. I had two mouthpieces. I was often played at feasts or funerals. You would play me by blowing.

I was often played with songs of joy. I can be played with one hand. You would play me by shaking me or tapping me.

I was made of metal. There were two parts to me, one of me for each hand. You would play me by clapping these two parts together.

Cymbals

Khalil: the pipe or flute

Shophar: ram's horn

Kinnor: the lyre

Nebel: the harp

Toph: the tambourine

Worshiping With Prayer

Scripture

"Come, let us bow down in worship, let us kneel before the Lord our Maker." Psalm 95:6

Goal

Learn that prayer is one way to worship God.

INTRODUCTION

You will need plain white paper, several blue and red colored pencils for the students to share, and three or four 8 1/2-by-11-inch pieces of red cellophane. (You could use clear, red plastic report covers instead.) Write the Scripture for today on a piece of paper or poster board or on the chalkboard so the students can see it and copy it.

As the students arrive, give each student a piece of paper. Ask the students to write the Scripture for today with the blue pencil. Tell them they should write lightly and not press too hard. Then over that, have them write any message they want with the red pencil. (The red message could be a note to a friend or a grocery list or the beginning of a story. The goal is to make the blue Scripture very difficult to decipher.) Now let the students take turns placing their message under the red cellophane. The red message will disappear, leaving the "secret Scripture" clearly visible.

DISCOVERY RALLY

Gather the students together in a large group.

WHAT'S THE GOOD WORD?

Choose a student to read the Scripture for today.

THE CHALLENGE

Ask: **Have you ever sent a secret message using the method we used with the Scripture in the introductory activity? What other kinds of codes do people use to communicate (secret or not)? Some people use sign language. Our alphabet is a code that most of us learn to read. Even math is a code: 2 + 2 is the code for 4. What are some other codes for 4?** (5 - 1, 1 + 3). **Why would people use secret codes to communicate?** (These people have a message that's meant only for certain other people to see or hear.) **Likewise, our prayers are meant for God to hear. And God hears not only our words, but also the feelings we don't have words for. Prayers are one way that we worship. Prayers are one way to express our wonder and love for God to God.** Tell the students that today in their Discovery Centers they will learn more about prayer as a way to worship.

PRAYER

DISCOVERY CENTERS

1. PRAY, PRAY, EVERY DAY

DO: Choose two students to sit on the floor facing each other. Instruct one of these students to hold one end of each yardstick in each hand. Have the other student hold the opposite ends of the yardsticks in each hand so that the yardsticks bridge the gap between them. Then ask the students holding the yardsticks to start a fairly slow rhythm of tapping the thin edges of the yardsticks on the floor about two feet apart, then tapping them again next to each other: apart, together, apart, together. While this rhythm is going on, ask one student to stand next to the moving

MATERIALS
two yardsticks

yardsticks with her side toward them. Instruct this student to hop in the same rhythm as the sticks, alternating feet: hop on left foot, hop on right foot, hop on left foot, and so on. (As the yardsticks are apart, the student's foot closest to the yardsticks should hop in the space between the sticks. As the sticks tap together, the student hops on the other foot.) As the student hops in this way, lead everyone in saying the following rhyme together. (The x's show where the student's foot hops between the opening between the yardsticks. The dots show where the student hops on the other foot.)

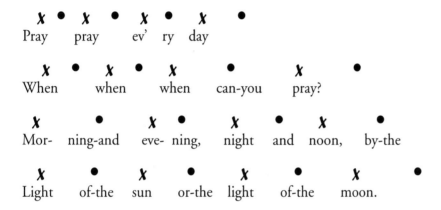

The object of the game is for the student to see if she can keep hopping all the way through the rhyme. If the student stops or gets "caught" by the sticks as they close, then it's the next student's turn. Encourage the students with the sticks to slow down or speed up according to the abilities of the group.

DISCUSS: What is prayer? (Prayer is talking to God with spoken words or with thoughts.) What makes prayer worship? (Worship means expressing our wonder and love for God to God.) It is making God the most important part of our lives. And there's no better way of showing people that they're important to you than spending time with them. Prayer is spending time with God, just the two of you together. It's a wonderful way to worship.

2. PRAYING GOD'S NAMES

MATERIALS
copies of the Names of God handout
(page 62), copies of A Calligraphy Pattern
handout (page 63), paper, markers

DO: Give each student one copy of each of the two handouts. Also give each student a sheet of notebook paper. Ask each student to look through the names of God and choose one that he likes best. Then with a washable ink marker of any color, instruct the students to write the name by drawing the letters as they are shown on the calligraphy page.

DISCUSS: What is a compliment? Give each student a compliment. **When we compliment God, it's called praise, and that's a part of worship. If God were with us in a physical body, we might hug him to show our love. But God is spirit. So praising God in prayer is our way of hugging God, of expressing our love for him to him. Praying God's names is a way to praise God in prayer. We might pray something like this: "Dear God, I praise you, because you are Almighty. You are the Most High God. You are my Maker and my Healer. You are the Holy One."**

Ask the students to join you in worshiping God in prayer by taking turns praying, "I praise you, because you are _____." Have them fill in the blank with the name they have chosen to write on their paper.

3. PRAISING GOD AROUND THE WORLD

MATERIALS
copies of the Nations Praise handout
(page 64), crayons or markers

DO: Ask a student to read Revelation 15:4. Give each student a copy of the Nations Praise handout. Then let the students take turns reading a name of one of the nations on the page. After a student reads the name of the nation, say the words that mean "Praise the Lord" in that language. Ask the students to repeat it after you. Then ask the students to color in the flags using the color code at the bottom of the page.

DISCUSS: **Imagine what it might be like when Jesus comes back and we get to worship God with people of every tribe and language. All the languages will praise God at the same time!** Try this as a group by letting each student choose from the page the praise words she wants to say. When you count to three, everyone says their praise words all together. **How can we praise the Lord in prayer? Since prayer is talking to God and not about God, we could say, "I praise you, Lord."** Encourage the students to follow "I praise you, Lord" by telling God why they are praising him. For example, "I praise you, Lord, because you have made such a beautiful sky." Let the students take turns telling you what they would put after, "I praise you, Lord, because. . . ."

DISCOVERERS' DEBRIEFING

If you have time to review, gather as a large group and discuss your young discoverers' findings. Ask the following questions:

- **What is the most interesting thing you discovered today?**
- **What did you learn today that you didn't know before?**
- **What is prayer?**
- **What makes prayer worship?**
- **What is it called when we compliment God?**
- **How can we pray God's names?**
- **How can we praise the Lord in prayer?**

Review the Scripture for today.

Worship God in prayer, praying some of his names and complimenting him.

NAMES OF GOD

These are just some of the names of God used in the Bible.

PROVIDER

HOLY ONE

KING OF GLORY

LORD ALMIGHTY

MOST HIGH

MAKER

SHIELD

MIGHTY ONE

REDEEMER

FATHER

ETERNAL GOD

MAJESTIC GLORY

COMFORTER

GOD OF TRUTH

SAVIOR

CREATOR

ETERNAL KING

A CALLIGRAPHY PATTERN

These letters are written in the Chancery Italic Hand. To make it easier to copy, skip a line between each line of writing. Between words, leave a space that is about as wide as a letter. It takes lots of practice to do these letters well, and it helps to use a special calligraphy pen, so don't worry if the letters you copy don't look quite like these.

NATIONS PRAISE

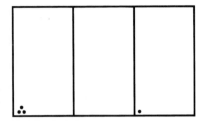

FRANCE
French: Gloire a Dieu
(glwar-ah-dyoo)

Color Key:

Red = •

Green = ••

Black = ✝

Yellow = ✗

Blue = ∴

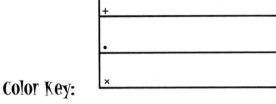

GERMANY
German: Prieze dem Herrn
(prize-dem-hairn)

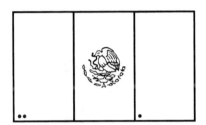

MEXICO
Spanish: Gloria a Dios
(glo-ree-ah-ah-dee-os)

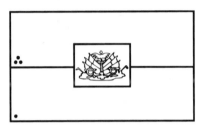

HAITI
Haitian: Bene Swala de Nea
(ben-ay-swah-la-duh-nay-ah)

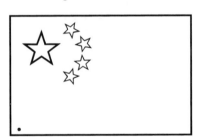

CHINA
Mandarin Chinese: Tsan Mai Shun
(tsoon-may-shoon)

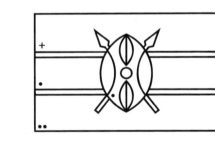

KENYA
Swahili: Bwana Asifiwe
(bwah-nah-ah-see-fee-way)

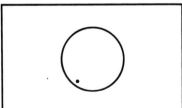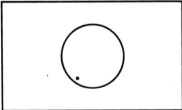

JAPAN
Japanese: Shuo homay tata ayo
(shoo-oh-ho-may-tah-tah-ay-oh)

JORDAN
Arabic: Mezhdan la Raab
(mezh-dahn-lah-rahb)

Worshiping With Communion

scripture

"On the night when Jesus was handed over to be killed, he took bread and gave thanks for it. Then he broke the bread and said, 'This is my body; it is for you. Do this to remember me.' In the same way, after they ate, Jesus took the cup. He said, 'This cup shows the new agreement from God to his people. This new agreement begins with the blood of my death. When you drink this, do it to remember me.'" 1 Corinthians 11:23-25, ICB

Goal

Learn that taking the Lord's Supper is one way to worship God.

NOTE: At the end of the lesson, you may wish to celebrate Communion with the students. If so, bring grape juice and unleavened bread or matzo crackers, and small paper cups.

INTRODUCTION *introduction*

Pour some washable purple paint onto several paper plates, just covering he bottom of each plate. As the students arrive, give each student a piece of white paper and a plastic communion cup. Tell the students to turn the cups upside down and press the rim of the cup into the purple paint. Then instruct them to press the rim of the cup onto paper, making a purple circle. Ask the students to paint a bunch of grapes on their papers by making lots of these purple circles close together.

DISCOVERY RALLY

Gather the students together in a large group.

WHAT'S THE GOOD WORD?

Choose a student to read the Scripture for today.

THE CHALLENGE

Ask: **What was in the cup that Jesus drank that night?** (Wine was in the cup.) **Why do you think Jesus used wine and not milk or water?** (The wine looks a bit like the blood that it represents.) **In Bible times wine was not only used as a drink, but also was used as a medicine and as a disinfectant (a cleanser).** Ask a student to read Isaiah 53:5. **Just as wine was used to heal, Jesus' blood also represents our healing.** Ask a student to read Hebrews 9:21, 22. **Just as wine was used as a cleanser, Jesus' blood represents the cleansing of our spirits from sin.** Tell the students that in their Discovery Centers today they will learn more about how Communion, the Lord's Supper, is a way to worship, to express our love for God to God.

PRAYER

DISCOVERY CENTERS

1. STORY STARTERS

DO: Spread your memory items out on the table in front of the students. Tell each of them to choose one that reminds them of something that happened to them. (For example, the birthday candle may re-mind one of them of a special birthday she had or a party a friend had.) Then let the students take turns using that object as a story starter, telling the brief true story of the occasion that the object brought to mind. After the students are fin-ished, show them the bread and juice. Point out to the students that they simply looked at the objects on the table and were reminded of things that had happened

MATERIALS

grape juice and communion bread or matzo crackers, objects that would remind students of occasions in their lives (valentine, Easter egg, Christmas ornament or card, birthday candle, gift bow, empty medicine bottle, sunglasses, ice cream cone, baseball, paintbrush)

in their lives. Jesus gave us something to look at, to touch, and to taste that would remind us of what he did for us.

DISCUSS: **What does Jesus want us to remember when we see and taste the bread and juice?** (Jesus wants us to remember that he gave his body and his blood to save us from sin, to bring us into God's kingdom.) **How can Communion (the Lord's Supper) be worship?** (When we take Communion, we show God that we remember his gift of salvation. We remember that Jesus is our Lord and Savior. We remember his death to forgive us of our sins. Worship is making God the most important person in our lives, and telling him so. Communion is part of telling him that he's most important.) **Can we worship Jesus as well as God the Father? Jesus is now at God's right hand, ruling in heaven** (Acts 5:31, Ephesians 1:19-21). **God told the angels to worship Jesus** (Hebrews 1:6). **Jesus is "the visible image of the invisible God"** (Colossians 1:15, NLT). **When we worship Jesus, we worship God.**

2. COMMUNION BREAD

DO: Ask the students to wash their hands. Then let the students measure and mix 1 cup of flour, 1/2 teaspoon salt, 1/4 cup cooking oil, and 2 1/2 tablespoons water. Give each student a paper plate to work on and divide the dough among the students. Ask them to pat their dough to be flat and thin. Then let them carefully write their initials in the dough. Bake these in your toaster oven at 450 degrees Fahrenheit for 10 to 12 minutes. If you have no toaster oven, arrange to bake this bread in your church's kitchen. (If neither option is convenient, let the students mix the dough and take it home in a sandwich bag. They can bake it at home. If you do this, you'll need to let the students copy the baking temperature and time on an index card.) Save the baked bread for taking Communion at the end of the session. Let the students wash their hands again.

> **MATERIALS**
> flour, salt, cooking oil, water, mixing bowl, measuring spoons, 1-cup dry measuring cup, 1-cup liquid measuring cup, mixing spoon, baking pan, pot holder, toothpicks, paper plates, toaster oven

DISCUSS: **What is the difference between communion bread and regular bread?** (This bread doesn't have any leavening or yeast in it to make it rise and puff up like regular bread. This bread stays flat.) Ask the students to remember the Scripture for today. **The reason Jesus ate flat bread that night was because he was eating the Passover meal with his friends. The flat bread was eaten at Passover to remind**

God's people of something very important. Ask a student to read Exodus 12:39. **The bread reminded God's people of how God had saved them from Egypt. When Jesus took the bread that night, what did he want it to remind us of?** (He wanted to remind us of how God has saved us from sin.) **As we think seriously about this when we eat the bread and drink the juice, we are worshiping.**

3. COMMUNION SCRIPTURES

DO: Assign one of the following Scriptures to each student. Ask the students to turn to these Scriptures in their Bibles and read them silently. Tell them to ask you if they need help pronouncing a word or understanding the Scripture. When they've finished, record each student in turn as he reads the Scripture. Accompany each reading with music if possible. Each student reads only one of the Scriptures. Continue taping on the same tape for your next group. (If you get to the end of the list before all of the students in your third group have a chance to read, turn to the crucifixion account in Matthew 27:32-54 and assign verses from this passage.)

MATERIALS
audio-cassette recorder, blank audio cassette, easy-to-read Bibles (ICB, NIrV, NLT, CEV), a musical instrument you play or an instrument and volunteer accompanist

Isaiah 53:3	Isaiah 53:4	Isaiah 53:5
Isaiah 53:6	Isaiah 53:7	Isaiah 53:8
Isaiah 53:9	Isaiah 53:10	Isaiah 53:11
Isaiah 53:12	Matthew 26:26	Matthew 26:27, 28
Romans 3:23, 24	Romans 3:25	Romans 6:6
Romans 6:7, 8	Romans 6:9	Romans 6:10
Philippians 2:6-8	Philippians 2:9-11	Colossians 1:18
Colossians 1:19, 20	Colossians 1:21, 22	

If you are going to celebrate Communion at the end of this session, play this tape as you take the bread and juice.

DISCUSS: What do you think about as you listen to these Scriptures? Thinking about Jesus' death as we take Communion helps us focus on who God is and what he has done. He is our loving Father who has saved us from sin. Thinking about these things (meditating) is one way to worship. It's one way to express our love for God to God.

If you have time, play back what the students have just recorded.

NOTE: If you don't have time to play this recording back to the students now or during the debriefing time to follow, bring the tape back next week to use during one of next week's activities.

DISCOVERERS' DEBRIEFING

If you have time, gather as a large group. Celebrate Communion by sharing the grape juice and the unleavened bread while listening to the tape that the students recorded during Discovery Center #3.

If you have more time, discuss your young discoverers' findings. Ask the following questions:

- **What is the most interesting thing you discovered today?**
- **What did you learn today that you didn't know before?**
- **What is Communion or the Lord's Supper?**
- **How can Communion be worship?**
- **What is it we are telling God by taking Communion?**

Review the Scripture for today.

Pray, thanking God for sending Jesus to save us from sin. Ask God to help us remember how important Communion is, and to help us grow in our understanding of what Jesus' death really means to us.

Worshiping by Reading God's Word

Scripture

"Oh, how I love your law! I think about it all day long. Your commands make me wiser than my enemies, for your commands are my constant guide." Psalm 119:97, 98, NLT

Goal

Learn that reading the Bible can be a way to worship God.

INTRODUCTION

On a chalkboard or poster board, write the first part of the Scripture for today ("Oh, how I love your law! I think about it all day long"). Display this so that the students can see it. Set out a stack of old magazines and newspapers that would be appropriate for students to look through. As the students arrive, give each one a piece of paper and ask them to cut out words and letters from different places in the newspapers and magazines, and glue them onto the paper to spell out the Scripture for today.

DISCOVERY RALLY

Gather the students together in a large group.

WHAT'S THE GOOD WORD?

Choose a student to read the Scripture for today.

THE CHALLENGE

Ask: **What does it mean to meditate?** It means to think deeply about something over and over again. Some people who don't believe in God read the Bible only for the purpose of learning about ancient civilizations and their customs. Some people who don't believe in God read the Bible as if it were a book of fables or wise words. **What is the difference in these people and the person who wrote the Scripture for today?** (That writer obviously thought deeply about God's Word over and over again.) **Why do you think this writer loved God's Word?** (This writer let God's Word draw him to God.) Ask a student to read John 5:39, 40. **What does this tell us about the purpose of the Bible, God's Word?** Tell the students that today, they will learn more about how to worship while reading God's Word.

PRAYER

DISCOVERY CENTERS

1. RED LETTERS

DO: Write "I know that you can do all things" (Job 42:2) on a chalkboard so that your group can see it. Give each student paper, a red pen, and a different color of pen. Ask the students to use the color other than red, and write this verse six times on the page. Then instruct them to go back to the first writing of the verse and copy over the word "I" with the red color. Tell them to go to the second writing and copy over the word "know" with red. On the third writing, they should copy over the word "you." On the fourth, they copy over the word "do." On the fifth, they copy over the word "all," and on the sixth they copy over the word "things."

MATERIALS
red pens, pens of another color, paper

DISCUSS: This is one way to meditate on God's Word. Emphasizing a different word each time we think about the verse helps us think deeply about it. When we think deeply about God's Word, we begin to feel an awe and love for God rising up in our hearts.

Ask the students to try it with you now. Talk about each writing, prompting the students' thoughts in the following way:

"I know that you can do all things." Who knows? Your mom or dad? Your teacher? No, you.

"I know . . ." Not I guess. Not I imagine. Not I think. I know. How do you know? What does it mean to know?

"I know that you . . ." Who was Job talking to when he said this? He was talking to God. "I know that God can do all things." Not me. Not the government. Not scientists. Not parents or teachers. God.

"I know that God can do . . ." Doing is active. Is it easier to think up something or to do something? Do is certain and complete. You either do something or you don't. God can do.

"I know that God can do all . . ." Does that mean a few things? Some things? Many things? How many is all? What is left out of all? What does all include?

"I know that God can do all things." What are things? Big, little, visible, invisible, feelings, objects, jobs, problems, happenings. Things are "whatever." God can do "whatever."

Now as you keep meditating, apply it to life. What does this verse mean to you in your life?

2. RESPONSIVE READINGS

MATERIALS

audio cassette recorded at Discovery Center #3 of Session 9 or a blank audio cassette and copies of the Worshiping With the Word handout (page 75), audio tape recorder

If you didn't listen to the tape recorded last week:
Ask the students to listen to the recording of the Scriptures they made last week. Ask them to meditate on the words as they are said. In other words, have them think deeply about these words, thinking about God's great gift to us through Jesus.

If you listened to the tape last week:
Give each student a copy of the Worshiping With the Word handout. Divide the students into two groups. Tell the students you are going to record a responsive reading with them. (That means that Group 1 will read the verses that are written in dark, bold letters. Group 2 will read the verses that are written in plain type.) Have the groups read this page once or twice for practice, and then tape it. After the tape has been made, listen to it. Ask the students to meditate on these words as they hear them. Ask them to think about God's great love and his plan for us.

DISCUSS: What does it mean to meditate? How can reading and meditating on Bible verses be worship? (These verses can help us feel wonder and love for God.) Tell me what these verses tell you about God. What kinds of feelings do you have when you read and hear these verses?

3. WORSHIP POSTERS

MATERIALS

copies of the Names of Jesus handout (page 76), half- or quarter-sheet pieces of white or light-colored poster board, markers or crayons

DO: Give each student a piece of poster board and a copy of the handout. Ask the students to write across the top of the poster, "He will be called." Across the bottom of the poster, they should write, "and he has called me friend." Then have them choose some of the names from the page to write at random across their poster. Encourage them to be creative, writing diagonally, horizontally, or vertically, with large letters or small, cursive or printed, plain or fancy. Tell them that these posters are for their own use.

DISCUSS: These words can be found in the Bible as descriptions of Jesus. The Bible also tells us that Jesus calls us his friends if we believe and follow him. When we come across these descriptions in our Bible reading, we can worship with them, meditating on what they mean. As the students work, comment on some of the names they chose from the list. For example, "I see that you've chosen the name Wonderful, Julie. What is it about Jesus that is wonderful to you?" Or, "You've chosen one of my favorites, Brian: Faithful. How has Jesus shown himself faithful to you?" As teacher, feel free to make a poster yourself or tell the students which name is most special to you and why. Tell the students that what they are doing now is meditating on God's Word as it describes Jesus.

DISCOVERERS' DEBRIEFING

If you have time to review, gather as a large group and discuss your young discoverers' findings. Ask the following questions:

- **What is the most interesting thing you discovered today?**
- **What did you learn today that you didn't know before?**
- **What is meditating?**
- **How can the reading of God's Word be worship?**

Review the Scripture for today.

Pray, thanking God for his Word, and asking him to help you worship with his Word.

WORSHIPING WITH THE WORD

How we praise God, the Father of our Lord Jesus Christ, who has blessed us with every spiritual blessing in the heavenly realms because we belong to Christ.

Long ago, even before he made the world, God loved us and chose us in Christ to be holy and without fault in his eyes.

His unchanging plan has always been to adopt us into his own family by bringing us to himself through Jesus Christ.

And this gave him great pleasure.

So we praise God for the wonderful kindness he has poured out on us because we belong to his dearly loved Son.

When you believed in Christ, he identified you as his own by giving you the Holy Spirit, whom he promised long ago.

The Spirit is God's guarantee that he will give us everything he promised and that he has purchased us to be his own people.

This is just one more reason for us to praise our glorious God.

For we are God's masterpiece. He has created us anew in Christ Jesus, so that we can do the good things he planned for us long ago.

May you have the power to understand, as all God's people should, how wide, how long, how high, and how deep his love really is.

May you experience the love of Christ, though it is so great you will never fully understand it.

Then you will be filled with the fullness of life and power that comes from God.

Ephesians 1:3-6, 13, 14; 2:10; 3:18, 19, NLT

NAMES OF JESUS

Alpha and Omega	Lamb of God	Son of Man
Ancient of Days	Light of Life	Teacher
Anointed One	Light of the World	First and Last
Bridegroom	Lord of Glory	Good Shepherd
Chief Cornerstone	Lord of Lords	Living One
Chief Shepherd	Prince of Peace	One and Only
Lord	Master	True Light
Faithful and True	Messiah	Truth
God's Son	Morning Star	The Way
Holy and Righteous One	Friend	The Word
Holy One of God	Intercessor	Bread of Life
Hope of Israel	Our Peace	The Vine
Immanuel (God with us)	Physician	Word of God
Savior	Righteous One	Wonderful
King of Kings	Rock Eternal	Counselor

Worship Through Dance and Art

Scripture

"David . . . danced before the Lord with all his might."
2 Samuel 6:14

Goal

Learn that dance and art can be expressions of love and worship toward God.

INTRODUCTION

You will need one copy of the Names of Jesus handout (Session 10, page 76) and one copy of the Names of God handout (Session 8, page 62). You will also need a plain, white handkerchief for each student, fabric markers, and old newspapers.

Spread the old newspapers over the work surface. As the students arrive, give each one a handkerchief. Tell each of them to look at the handouts and choose one of the names of God or Jesus to write on the handkerchief. Then ask them to design decorative borders around it. (These will be used as worship banners in Discovery Center #3.)

DISCOVERY RALLY

Gather the students together in a large group.

WHAT'S THE GOOD WORD?

Choose a student to read the Scripture for today.

THE CHALLENGE

Ask: **How many of you have ever been to a football game, baseball game, or basketball game or have watched these on TV? What do the fans do when their team makes a touchdown, a homerun, or a basket?** (People jump up and down. They clap and shout.) **How many of you have ever been with preschool children when the children are excited? What do they do?** (They dance around and jump up and down and clap.) **What did David do when he was excited about the ark of God coming to the worship tent? Today's Scripture tells us. What does it mean when it says he danced "before the Lord"? Was he dancing just for the fun of it? Was he dancing so everyone could see what a good dancer he was? No. He was dancing for God. He was worshiping. He was expressing his wonder and love for God, to God.** Tell the students that today in their Discovery Centers they will learn about worshiping God through dance and art.

PRAYER

DISCOVERY CENTERS

1. HAND DANCING

MATERIALS
copies of the Psalm 148 handout
(page 81)

DO: Ask if anyone in the group takes dance lessons. If they do, ask them to show some of the hand positions or other hand movements they use in dance.
Then give the students the hand signs for Psalm 148. Read verses 1, 3, 4, 7-12. Practice the signs together.

DISCUSS: We usually don't think of hand signs as dancing, but they can be.

This is "hand dancing," a way to worship. How can this be worship? (Worship is expressing our wonder and love for God, to God.) **If we are not thinking about God when we do hand signs, it's just signing. But if we are doing it for God, to God, then it is worship.**

2. PASTELS AND SCULPTURES

MATERIALS
Bible, audio cassette or CD of instrumental worship music and a tape or CD player, large pieces of manila paper or sketch paper from an art pad, pastels (colored chalk), buttermilk or liquid fabric starch, disposable paper bowls, modeling clay, old newspapers

DO: Tell the students that they are going to worship God with visual art today. Tell them they can choose to paint with pastels or to sculpt with clay. Cover the work areas with old newspapers. Let the students get the tools for the medium of their choice. For those who choose to paint with pastels, give them each a bowl and pour about 1/2 inch of buttermilk or liquid starch into it. Tell them that before they begin drawing, they should dip the pastel into the liquid. They can dip it into the liquid as often as they need to. Tell them that there is no right or wrong method to make what they create. It can be realistic or it can be an abstract design. Also tell the students to think about God as they work and to create a painting or sculpture to honor him. Then turn to Revelation 21. Turn on the worship music and begin reading aloud. The students should begin sculpting or painting as you read. Read Revelation 21, 22, or as much of these as you can.

DISCUSS: **What did you feel as you thought about God and worked on your art?** Let the students show what they made. **How can art be worship?** (Worship is expressing our wonder and love for God and to God.) **When we do this with our art, we are worshiping.**

3. BANNER DANCING

MATERIALS
musical instrument and someone to play it, banners from introductory activity

DO: Ask the students to stand in a circle with the banners they made during the introductory activity. Have each student hold two adjacent corners of her banner. Choose one student to be the leader. Tell the other students to follow this student around the circle. Tell the students that this will be similar to Follow the Leader, but as they move about, they are to think about honoring God. This creative movement is their gift to God at this time. If the students seem unsure, be the first leader to show them what to do. Show them that they can skip, twirl, hop, march, wave their banners, stand in place and do what we might normally call "exercises" (the windmill, jumping jacks, toe touches). Play music as the students dance. You can sing a worship song if you want. You can also play an audio cassette or CD of worship music or use the music coming from Discovery Center #2 if it's loud enough.

DISCUSS: **What makes the difference between a worship dance and any other kind of dance?** Ask a student to read the Scripture for today. **Why did David dance?** (He danced to honor God.) **How can dancing be worship?** (Worship is expressing our wonder and love for God, to God.) **When dance expresses our wonder and love for God, to God, it's worship.**

DISCOVERERS' DEBRIEFING

If you have time to review, gather as a large group and discuss your young discoverers' findings. Ask the following questions:
  • **What is the most interesting thing you discovered today?**
  • **What did you learn today that you didn't know before?**
  • **Why did David dance?**
  • **What makes the difference between worship dances and other kinds of dances?**
  • **How can art be worship?**

Review the Scripture for today.

Pray, thanking God for giving us hearts that enjoy expressing themselves in many different ways. Thank God for art and dance, and ask him to help us know how to worship him better.

PSALM 148

Praise

the Lord,

sky

Praise the
Lord
(as above)

sun

and rain

Praise the
Lord
(as above)

tree

and animals

(hands on chest,
rock in and out
sideways)

Praise the
Lord
(as above)

old people

and children

Giving as Worship

Scripture

"You will be glorifying God through your generous gifts." 2 Corinthians 9:13, NLT

Goal

Learn that giving expresses our love to God.

INTRODUCTION

As the students arrive, ask each of them to get a piece of colored construction paper (any color), trace around both their hands, and cut out the hand tracings. Draw a large circle on a piece of poster board. Ask each student to tape or glue his hand-print to the drawn circle so that together everyone's handprints make a wreath shape.

DISCOVERY RALLY

Gather the students together in a large group.

WHAT'S THE GOOD WORD?

Choose a student to read the Scripture for the day.

THE CHALLENGE

Tell the students that today they will be learning about how giving can be worship. It can show your love for God, to God. Ask the students to make fists with both of their hands. Ask: **Have you ever heard the words "tightfisted" or "closefisted?" These are words that mean "stingy" or "selfish."** Ask them to open their hands. **"Openhanded" is a word that is sometimes used to mean "generous" or "giving." This is what the hands on the wreath mean. They mean that we are generous, giving people.** Tell the students that in their Discovery Centers today they will learn more about giving as a way of worship.

PRAYER

DISCOVERY CENTERS

1. GIFT BASKETS

MATERIALS
4-by-6-inch index cards, paper punch, scissors, colorful yarn

DO: Give each student four index cards. Ask them to cut only one card in half. Then punch four holes along the long sides of each card, not including the card cut in half. Then punch two holes along the short sides of each card, including each side of the two halves. Now give each student about 12 inches of yarn. Have the students lay the cards out as shown on page 84 and "sew" through the holes of the side cards and into the holes of the center card (which becomes the bottom of the basket). Then have them raise the sides up, one at a time, and sew the sides together, weaving the yarn in and out of the holes. If they run out of yarn, just tie on another piece and keep going.

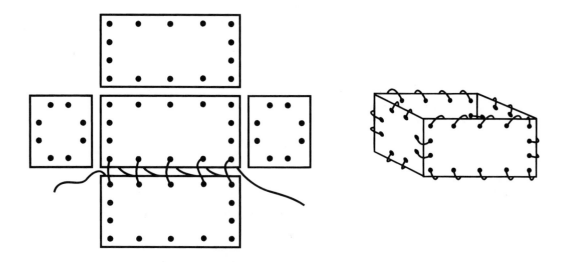

Your first two groups should take their baskets with them to use in Discovery Center #3. Your third group will bring potpourri with them from the Discovery Center and will need to place these bags into their baskets. Ask them to whom they plan to give their gift basket.

DISCUSS: As the students work, tell them that this basket will be a gift to someone. **Think of a person you want to give it to. What are some occasions on which we give gifts? What do gifts tell the people who receive them? How can we give to God?** Ask a student to read Matthew 25:31-40. **What does this tell us about giving to God? How can giving be worship?** It is a way of expressing our thankfulness and love for God, to God.

2. FIRSTFRUITS

MATERIALS
paper, pencils

DO: Give each student a piece of paper. Ask the students to write their names at the top of their pages. Then ask them to draw a symbol of some talent that God has given them. (For example, if they are good singers, they could draw a musical note. If they play piano, they could draw a piano or a keyboard. If they are good at sports, they could draw a symbol of that sport.) If the student doesn't seem to know what she is good at, ask what that student enjoys doing. This might give a clue to her talents, because usually we enjoy doing things that we are talented at doing. As teacher, you should also make a drawing.

After the students have finished their drawings, ask them to place the drawings in their outstretched palms as if serving someone. Then ask the students to join you in lifting these gifts up toward God as you lead them in prayer. Thank God for giving you these gifts and talents. Tell God that you dedicate these gifts to him so that he will receive the glory and honor for all the talents you have.

DISCUSS: **How can you use your talents and gifts to honor God? How can this be worship?** (We will make choices about our talents by asking God what he wants us to do. We will think about what will honor God and bring him glory. Using our talents in this way will show God that he comes first in our lives.) **It is an expression of our thankfulness and love for God. That's worship.**

3. BASKET POTPOURRI

MATERIALS

whole stick cinnamon, whole cloves, dried orange peels, ground cinnamon, ground cloves, mixing bowl, mixing spoon, small disposable picnic bowls, 3-by-5-inch index cards, paper punch, pens and markers, narrow ribbon or yarn cut into 6-inch sections, plastic sandwich bags

DO: Ask your first group to divide the ingredients evenly into groups of three using the small bowls. One of these three bowls of ingredients will be used for each of your groups.

Now instruct the students in your group to break their cinnamon sticks and orange peel into smaller pieces. Then mix the cinnamon sticks, orange peel, cloves (whole and ground), and ground cinnamon. Give each student a sandwich bag. Divide the mixture evenly among the students. Then ask each student to write on an index card, "Cover with water and simmer. Add more water as needed." Then punch a hole in the corner of each card, thread the ribbon or yarn through it, and tie the ribbon or yarn around the top of the plastic bag to close it securely. If this is your second or third group, have them place the bag in the gift basket they made at Discovery Center #1. If this is your first group, they will take the potpourri with them to the Discovery Center where they will make a basket. Ask the students to whom they will give this gift.

DISCUSS: Ask a student to read Proverbs 14:31. **What does this tell us about giving? Is giving always an act of worship? What are some reasons people give to each other?** (To get something in return, because it's a holiday or a tradition, to get rid of something they don't want, because someone else makes them give something, or because they are expressing love or honor.) **How could a person give money at church and not be worshiping as they give? What makes giving a part of worship?** (When it expresses thankfulness and love to God, it is worship.)

DISCOVERERS' DEBRIEFING

If you have time to review, gather as a large group and discuss your young discoverers' findings. Ask the following questions:

- **What is the most interesting thing you discovered today?**
- **What did you learn today that you didn't know before?**
- **What are some different reasons that people give?**
- **What makes giving worship?**
- **Why does God want us to give?**

Review the Scripture for today.

Pray about giving ourselves and our talents to God for his glory. Ask God to help us make giving a way of worship, an expression of our love to him.

Leading Worship

Scripture

"Come, let us sing for joy to the Lord; let us shout aloud to the Rock of our salvation. " Psalm 95:1

Goal

Learn that some people are gifted at leading others in worshiping together. Learn how to lead others in worshiping together.

INTRODUCTION

As the students arrive, divide them into pairs. Ask the two to stand facing each other. Ask one partner to be the Leader and the other to be the Follower. Instruct the Leader to make slow deliberate movements, and tell the Follower to copy the movements as exactly as possible, trying to be a mirror image. After a few minutes of this, have them switch. (Leader becomes Follower, and Follower becomes Leader.) If you have time after this, switch partners and do the same thing again.

DISCOVERY RALLY

Gather the students together in a large group.

WHAT'S THE GOOD WORD?

Choose a student to read the Scripture for today.

THE CHALLENGE

Ask: **What do you think are the biggest fears of most people? A survey taken several years ago showed that the ten worst fears in the United States were (from least feared to most feared)**

    10. dogs

     9. loneliness

     8. flying

     7. death

     6. sickness

     5. deep water

     4. not having enough money

     3. insects and bugs

     2. heights

     1. speaking in front of a group

Go back through the list and ask the students to raise their hands if they have this particular fear. **Why might people be most afraid of speaking in front of a group? God gave some people the skill and ability to lead groups.** In their Discovery Centers today, they will learn about leading worship. Tell them that they will stay in the same Discovery Centers for the length of two group times. Then they will come together in a large group for worship.

NOTE: Divide your groups into three centers as usual. But all three centers will do the same activities at the same time. There will be two activities. Then the groups will combine for worship.

PRAYER

DISCOVERY CENTERS

All three discovery groups will do the following activity first.

1. DISCOVERING LEADERS

DO: Cut out each description and its questions from a copy of Discovering Leaders. Give each student a Bible, a pencil, and one of these description slips. Ask the students to turn to the reference listed on their description slip and write the answer to the question on the slip. Help students if needed. After they have all answered their questions, ask the students to read their description slips along with what they discovered about this leader.

MATERIALS
copies of Discovering Leaders (pages 92-94),
scissors, pencils, Bibles

DISCUSS: Did all the leaders feel qualified for the job that God asked them to do? Why or why not? Did you ever feel as though you didn't know how to lead, or you weren't good enough at the job to lead? Are you a leader of anything at school? If so, tell about it. Who gives the ability to lead? Sometimes we don't know we can lead until we try it. Why do people need leaders? What attitude does God like to see in leaders? (Courage, trust/dependence on God, humility, willingness to serve.)

All three discovery groups will do the following activity second.

2. PLANNING FOR WORSHIP

DO: Ask one student to be the secretary for the group. Have a chalkboard, white board or poster board available for the secretary to write on. Then ask the group to list some ways God's people worship when they come together. (They need not list all of the following, but here are some choices: prayer, music and singing, giving, Communion, Scripture reading, dance, art, meditating on God's Word.) As the students list ways to worship corporately, the secretary should write the ways on the board.

MATERIALS
chalkboard, white board, or poster board

Tell the students that the group is now going to plan for worship time and that the theme of the worship time will be thankfulness. Go down the list of ways to worship that the students just made. Ask for a volunteer to pray when the large group comes together. If no one volunteers and you know a student who would do it if you ask, then ask that student. Take suggestions from the group about what a thankful prayer might include. Then ask for a volunteer to lead a song. Ask the group to suggest a song that would express thanks or praise to God. Then ask for someone to read a Scripture. Ask for Scripture suggestions. If no one has an idea, have each group choose from one of the following lists.

Ask the first group to choose from these verses:
>   Psalm 7:17
>   Psalm 28:6, 7
>   Psalm 100

Ask the second group to choose from these verses:
>   Psalm 105:1-4
>   Psalm 118:24
>   Psalm 118:28, 29

Ask the third group to choose from these verses:
>   Revelation 7:11, 12
>   Psalm 136 (part or all; as a responsive reading if each student has a Bible.)

DISCUSS: Some worship times are spontaneous. That means that the leaders do not plan what to do, what to say, or what to sing. Instead, the leaders make those choices while they are leading by paying attention to what they think God is leading the group to do in worship. At other times, leaders plan what to do, just like we did. But they still try to think about what God wants the group to do in worship.

For this last activity, ask all the groups to come together to form one large group.

3. WORSHIP

DO: Bring all three groups together and let each group take a turn leading with a prayer, a song, and a Scripture. Then give the students the Praise Rounds handout and teach them these songs set to tunes they already know. After the students have sung the songs once or twice together, divide them into two or three groups and sing the songs as rounds.

MATERIALS
copies of Praise Rounds handout (page 95)

DISCOVERERS' DEBRIEFING

Discuss these questions after the worship time.

- **What is the most interesting thing you discovered today?**
- **What did you learn today that you didn't know before?**
- **What is worship?**
- **Do all worship leaders feel that they are qualified to lead?**
- **Why are some people afraid to lead others?**
- **Do you feel that you are a leader or a follower?**
- **If you are a leader, what gift has God given you to lead?**

Review the Scripture for today.

Pray, asking God to show us where he wants us to lead and where he wants us to follow. Ask him to help us be bold but humble leaders and followers.

DISCOVERING LEADERS

MY NAME IS MOSES.

Read Exodus 4:10-17 to find out:

What did I say when God told me to be a leader? _____

_____

What did God do then? _____

_____

MY NAME IS GIDEON.

Read Judges 6:15, 16 to find out:

What did I say when God told me to be a leader? _____

_____

What did God say then? _____

_____

MY NAME IS JEREMIAH.

Read Jeremiah 1:4-10 to find out:

What did I say when God told me to be a leader? _____

_____

What did God say then? _____

_____

MY NAME IS HEMAN.

Read 1 Chronicles 6:31-48 to find out:

What was my job? _____

_____

Who were my assistants? _____

_____

Where did we work? _____

_____

WE WERE MUSICIANS.

Read 1 Chronicles 9:33, 34 to find out:

Where did we live? _____

_____

What hours were we on duty? _____

_____

WE WERE LEVITE LEADERS.

Read 1 Chronicles 15:16-22 to find out:

Who chose us? _____

_____

What was Kenaniah chosen to do and why? (See verse 22.) _____

_____

WE LED WORSHIP BEFORE THE ARK OF THE LORD.

Read 1 Chronicles 16:1-6 to find out:

What kinds of instruments did we play? _____

_____

_____

WE WERE MUSICIANS AT THE HOUSE OF THE LORD.

Read 1 Chronicles 25:6-8 to find out:

Whose direction were we under? _____

_____

What were we trained to do? _____

_____

How many of us were there? _____

_____

Were we young or old, or both? _____

_____

MY NAME IS MATTANIAH.

Read Nehemiah 11:17 to find out:

What was my job? _____

_____

Read Nehemiah 11:23 to find out:

Who gave us orders about what to do? _____

_____

WE WERE CHOIR DIRECTORS.

Read Nehemiah 12:46, 47 to find out:

What kinds of songs did we lead? _____

_____

How did we get enough food to eat? (Some Bibles call food "daily portion" in this
verse.) _____

_____

PRAISE ROUNDS

LORD, WE WORSHIP YOU

(Tune: "Row, Row, Row Your Boat")

Lord, we worship you,
Following your ways.
You're the King of Kings.
You deserve all praise.

ONLY YOU

(Tune: "Are You Sleeping?")

You are my God.
You are my God.
I love you.
I love you.
You alone are worthy.
You deserve all glory.
Only you.
Only you.

PERFECT GOD

(Tune: "Three Blind Mice")

Perfect God, perfect God,
Holy King, Holy King,
You're the Savior that we adore,
Prince of Peace and Lord of Lords,
Mighty Ruler and Living Word.
We praise you, Lord.
We praise you, Lord.